THE
ADVERSITY
ADVANTAGE

Turning Everyday Struggles into Everyday Greatness

DELUXE EDITION
Updated with New Stories from
the Seven Summits and Expedition Photographs

Paul G. Stoltz, Ph.D., and Erik Weihenmayer

A FIRESIDE BOOK
PUBLISHED BY SIMON & SCHUSTER

NEW YORK   LONDON   TORONTO   SYDNEY

Fireside
A Division of Simon & Schuster, Inc.
1230 Avenue of the Americas
New York, NY 10020

This Fireside trade paperback edition August 2010

FIRESIDE and colophon are registered trademarks of Simon & Schuster, Inc.

For information about special discounts for bulk purchases,
please contact Simon & Schuster Special Sales at
1-866-506-1949 or business@simonandschuster.com.

The Simon & Schuster Speakers Bureau can bring authors to your live event.
For more information or to book an event contact the Simon & Schuster Speakers Bureau
at 1-866-248-3049 or visit our website at www.simonspeakers.com.

Manufactured in the United States of America

5 7 9 10 8 6

Library of Congress Cataloging-in-Publication Data
Stoltz, Paul Gordon.
The adversity advantage : turning everyday struggles into everyday greatness : updated with new stories from
the seven summits and expedition photographs / by Paul G. Stoltz & Erik Weihenmayer. — Deluxe ed.
        p.   cm.
Includes index.
1. Success—Psychological aspects.   2. Self-management (Psychology)
I. Weihenmayer, Erik.   II. Title.
BF637.S8S694 2010
158.1—dc22
2010021697

ISBN 978-1-4391-9949-7
ISBN 978-0-7432-9931-2 (ebook)

We dedicate this book to my beloved brother,
Mark Weihenmayer (1959–2006),
and to those like Mark who face adversity every day,
yearning for the tools to emerge stronger and better.
May adversity become the pathway through which you flourish.
Your greatness is needed.

—ERIK WEIHENMAYER

Contents

Foreword

STEPHEN R. COVEY

Many years ago, I was wandering around the stacks of a library and a book by Dr. Viktor Frankl caught my attention. What I read was so inspiring, so compelling, and so profound that it changed my life. I memorized these three sentences:

> Between stimulus and response, there is a space.
> In that space lies our freedom and power to choose our response.
> In those choices lie our growth and our happiness.

Think about it—between the time that whatever has happened to you, or is now happening to you, and your response to that event, there is a moment in which you have the power and freedom to choose your response. Those chosen responses will govern your growth and your happiness. In fact, they will govern your achievements and your contributions.

In other words, we are not merely a product of our genetics, our conditioning, or our present circumstances. *The Adversity Advantage* is an in-depth exploration of the principle behind these three sentences that have had such a deep impact upon me.

This is not a theoretical book, even though there is extensive theorizing, nor is this a book full of abstract idealism, even though it shows how the ideal can become real. Instead, *The Adversity Advantage* is the synergistic product of two marvelous individuals who teamed up to share what they have learned from their respective experiences: Erik from the unique perspective of being the only blind person to climb the highest peak on the seven continents of the world, Paul from his life's work decoding and strengthening the human relationship with adversity. Their collaboration was much like an Everest climb—a grueling ascent through innumerable obstacles, culminating in this powerful message from the top of the world. Erik brought his insights from the mountains; Paul added his hard-won knowledge and helped Erik shape all those insights into a lesson plan for readers to help them achieve everyday greatness.

Not all greatness is the same. *Primary* greatness lies in character and in contribution. *Secondary* greatness is found in prestige, wealth, position, and the kinds of achievements that make no solid, lasting contribution to others. All of us want our children and grandchildren to develop primary greatness. They may also attain secondary greatness. But seldom do people achieve both. A few celebrities do, but most celebrities only achieve secondary greatness. Many everyday people achieve primary greatness, particularly parents who raise children of character and contribution.

There is one common trait found in all greatness: how people use the space between stimulus and response. In short, how do people deal with adversity, with setbacks, with suffering, heartache, disappointment, and injustice? Do they become victims, consumed by the metastasizing cancers of cynicism, criticizing, complaining, comparing, competing, and contending? Or do they learn to harness the power, energy, and wisdom embodied in the difficult moment?

How ironic that what enables us to grow and experience true joy in life is the very thing most people spend most of their lives trying to avoid. A life of convenience and comfort and pleasure is the path of least resistance and contributes nothing. I take as a mantra for life: grow or die. Keep learning and contributing . . . or die. I believe this is true, not just symbolically, but literally. When we stop growing and learning, we wither.

In his bestselling book, *Man's Search for Meaning*, Dr. Frankl helps others find meaning in their suffering, no matter how severe. He explains that someone who has a "why" can live with any "what" and any "how." His concept of dealing with adversity and achieving a deeper sense of purpose resonates in this book.

The remarkable thing about *The Adversity Advantage* is how applicable it is to every facet of life—physical, mental, social, emotional, economic, and spiritual. Want to make a real contribution? Pay the price. Invest yourself in a cause. Swim upstream against the cultural currents. Fight convention. Want to live a healthy, long life? Train smart. Stress your body, but don't overstress it. Participate in aerobics, strength training, and flexibility exercises. Eat wisely. Want to improve your relationships? See love as a verb, rather than as a feeling. Stop criticizing, finding fault, and blaming; instead serve, listen, and anticipate.

Businesspeople, do you want more customers? Give that extra mile of service. Go beyond what others do. Look on your customers' difficulties and problems, their adversities, as an opportunity where you can go way beyond what is normally expected. You'll get these customers for life.

Want to build a strong, trusting, highly productive culture in your organization with everyone focused on second-mile service? Use the adversity advantage. Get to know your people, listen to them, and understand their pains, their hopes, their desires, their problems, and their self-doubts. Be true to your team behind their backs when the easier way would be to join in with others in criticizing. If you are critical by nature, then learn to give them positive feedback. This will take courage, particularly if you do it in a humble—not an arrogant—way.

Want to grow spiritually? Let service be your mantra. Never

retire from meaningful work or projects. Where much is given, much is acquired. This kind of service will mean dealing with adversity on a daily basis, but as explained here, you'll learn to "take on" these challenges, "summon your strengths," "engage your CORE," and "pioneer possibilities." You'll learn to "pack light and right," "suffer well," and then "deliver" this kind of great service on a consistent, regular basis.

The powerful principles in this book represent the tallest mountains on the seven continents of the world. They are presented inductively so that you can *earn* the insights, not just *learn* them. Inductive thinking means moving from the specific to the general. Deductive means that you start with theory (general) and then begin to apply it to specific situations.

In *The Adversity Advantage*, each chapter, or Summit, starts with the specifics: a story about Erik's mountain experiences. Then the reader proceeds to general concepts offered by Dr. Paul Stoltz, who developed the Adversity Quotient—the most widely accepted method for assessing and strengthening our ability to deal with adversity. Over half a million people have measured their Adversity Quotient, or AQ, and begun the journey of strengthening how they deal with adversity. Dr. Stoltz has conducted groundbreaking research in nearly two dozen countries to gain an understanding of those rare people who don't merely deal well with adversity, but convert it into fuel to achieve greatness.

This book is filled with tools, principles, and challenges that are both practical and compelling. I found that reading *The Adversity Advantage* led me to look carefully at how my life challenges can be the very fuel that enables me to swim against the stream, against cultural currents, against all forms of adversity inherent in my most important goals.

Setbacks are inevitable, but misery is a choice.

The Adversity Advantage can help equip you to harness and utilize the hard moments to achieve the greatest heights of growth and contribution. That's where true happiness is found. This book gave me a real appreciation for adversity and helped me see greater possibilities. It has inspired me to be an alchemist, to turn lead into gold.

This is not a book you just quickly skim to get the main points. You have to earn those points by working with the knowledge and trying to internalize it. One of the best ways to learn this material is to teach the essence of the seven steps to your loved ones and others who might be interested.

I often ask audiences, "How many of you have achieved your present level of success, whatever it may be, partly or largely because someone believed in you when you didn't believe in yourself?" Usually about two-thirds of the audience members will raise their hands, and when you listen to some of them, you see tears shed by both speakers and listeners.

After a lifetime of tackling adversity head-on, and achieving greater successes than many sighted people, Erik sums up his insights: "I believe that inside each of us is something I can only describe as a light, which has the capacity to feed on adversity, to consume it like fuel. When we tap into that light, every frustration, every setback, every obstacle becomes a source to power our lives forward. The greater the challenge, the brighter the light burns. Through it, we become more focused, more creative, and more driven, and can even learn to transcend our own perceived limitations to bring our lives more meaning."

Between adversity and our response is a space. In that space are the power and freedom to choose to crumble, or to elevate both ourselves and others, as these two authors do by sharing their work with us. Dear reader, pay the price with this book. The dividends will be abundant and will last forever.

Stephen R. Covey is the author of the bestselling book *The 7 Habits of Highly Effective People.* His other books include *First Things First, Principle-Centered Leadership, The 7 Habits of Highly Effective Families, The 8th Habit,* and *The Leader in Me—How Schools and Parents Around the World Are Inspiring Greatness, One Child at a Time.*

Introduction

Erik

What if, as a result of completing this book, you could use any, and I mean *any,* adversity to your advantage? What if you could convert your everyday struggles, big and small, into the kind of fuel that powers you past everyday normality to everyday greatness?

Isn't there something incredibly riveting about the human struggle with adversity? Not only is it the thread strand of our story, shared across eras and cultures, but we also read about it in all of the great books, are spellbound by it in popular movies, and wrestle with it in our own lives every day. But why adversity?

Erik and Paul both contribute to this book, so their passages are differentiated by the use of a different typeface for each voice. This is Erik's text.

Maybe it's because within that struggle lies the essential wisdom we all need to become the kind of person we hope to be, or to grow the kind of team or organization we envision. In fact, after spending the past few years working on this book, I'm convinced that adversity holds the key to achieving everyday greatness in life, business, and society.

We don't have to go looking for adversity. It tends to find us. During the summer between eighth and ninth grades, I began losing the last traces of sight. I could no longer see enough to walk around by myself, so my brothers and parents had to lead me. I'd reach out for their shirtsleeves with the terror of a small child being left behind in a department store. I hated what was happening because it represented utter helplessness. Everything I knew was ending. The loss was like a storm descending upon me with such force, such viciousness, that I thought I'd be crushed by it.

Late that fall, I was watching the TV show *That's Incredible.* I could still see a little out of one eye, though I had to crane forward just a few inches away from the television. The feature story that night was about an athlete named Terry Fox. Terry had lost a leg to cancer and, when not yet discharged from the hospital, made a decision to run across Canada from east to west. With my nose pressed up against the screen, I watched Terry run—tears poured down my face. The miles took a tremendous toll on his amputated leg and its primitive prosthetic. He hobbled along, mile after mile, fighting the pain of blisters and raw skin, often using a pair of crutches to propel his body forward.

The look on his face struck me most. It was a look of extreme contradiction: full of exhaustion, yet radiant with exaltation. In his thin face was the trace flicker of an intense internal light that burned power into his struggling frame. The images filled my sagging spirit and gave me a feeling of utter courage. Many would have retreated from such hardship, but—surprisingly—Terry faced it head-on and literally ran into its midst. It was while staring into Terry's face that I first wondered how we could harness that great storm of adversity swirling around us and use its power to make ourselves stronger and better.

Although I was inspired by Terry, I learned early on that inspiration is

My hero, Terry Fox, had his right leg amputated due to bone cancer when he was eighteen years old, and while in the hospital, was so affected by the other children with cancer that he decided to run across Canada to raise money for cancer research. One of my last visual memories before going blind was Terry's face on a TV show, full of exhaustion yet radiant with exaltation, during his historic run. He made it 143 days and over 3,000 miles before he was forced to stop when the cancer reappeared in his lungs. He died in 1981 at just twenty-two, but his vision continues through dozens of annual Terry Fox Runs around the world.

not enough. If a person embarks on a mountain expedition unprepared and poorly equipped, the fierce wind, the frigid cold, and the steep terrain will do him in every time. Likewise, to consistently convert everyday adversity, big and small, into genuine advantage in our lives and enterprises we need powerful and proven tools. And no one is better qualified to teach us about those tools than the guy I teamed up with to write this book, Dr. Paul Stoltz.

Paul is perhaps best known for his Adversity Quotient, or AQ theory, which has become the most widely adopted method in the world for measuring and strengthening how we deal with adversity. Decoding the human relationship with adversity has been and continues to be Paul's life's work.

It was through Paul's groundbreaking research that we met. His focus on people who harness life's tough stuff led him to launch the Global Resilience Project, an effort now involving studies in twenty-one countries. His quest is to gain a better understanding of those rare people who don't just cope with adversity, but who learn to convert it into fuel to achieve everyday greatness.

I believe that inside each of us is something I can only describe as a light, which has the capacity to feed on adversity, to consume it like fuel. When we tap into that light, every frustration, every setback, every obstacle becomes a source to power our lives forward. The greater the challenge, the brighter the light burns. Through it, we become more focused, more creative, more driven, and can even learn to transcend our own perceived limitations to bring our lives more meaning.

You might remember, from your history textbooks, those medieval alchemists who toiled to mysteriously turn lead into gold. No one has yet figured out how to chemically transmute one metal into another but, on a figurative level, some people have successfully turned their trials and tribulations into priceless experiences. I call people like Terry, the people Paul has highlighted from his research, modern-day alchemists. All of us can be alchemists, taking the lead that life piles on top of us and finding ways to transform it into gold. I strive to be an alchemist every day. I climbed the Seven Summits—the tallest peaks on each of the seven continents—not only because I love to climb but also to shatter people's perceptions of what is possible. And somewhere along the way, I learned more about the advantages of adversity than I ever imagined I would.

There is something inherently compelling about an ascent. I believe that deep inside us, we all strive to move forward and up, to scale new heights. Paul and I have organized this book into Seven Summits, based on seven guiding principles that will help you use adversity to your advantage, as a way to infuse some practical greatness into your daily life. I begin each Summit—each chapter—with a story from one of the seven actual summits that I climbed. In between Paul draws from my lessons and his research to teach you how you can generate power from your everyday struggles, elevating you and everyone you touch.

Paul

Quitters, Campers, and Climbers

By "everyone," Erik and I hope you include your associates at work, your community, your family, and more. This is because the ripple effect—both positive and negative—of how you relate to adversity extends out to all whom you influence. That's the potential power of *The Adversity Advantage*, and it's why Erik and I love the word *elevate*. To elevate means to "raise to a higher level or position," or to "raise one's mind or spirit to a more enlightened or exalted level." And when it really comes down to it, isn't that what you want to do with your life, what every parent hopes to do for a child, what every leader wants to do for his or her organization?

You might be thinking that any sensible person seeks less adversity, not more. *Right?* Here's the problem. While you can certainly have an enjoyable life, you cannot reach beyond pleasure to even the most basic level of greatness without a healthy dose of the very thing most people seek to diminish. Why? Because adversity alone has the unique power to inspire exceptional clarity, purge any vestiges of lethargy, refocus your priorities, hone your character, and unleash your most potent forces. Even minor setbacks provide powerful opportunities for elevating behavior. If you eliminate adversity, you miss out on life's deepest riches, highest gifts, and most potent lessons. The more adversity you escape, the less you become. You cannot elevate anyone or anything to its highest potential without adversity.

Your Adversity Quotient (AQ) is a measure of how you respond to adversity of all kinds, or how you react to the world around you. In my first books introducing AQ, I talked in depth about Quitters, Campers, and Climbers—the three categories of response to the daunting challenge of leading an ever-elevating life.

- *Quitters* simply give up on the ascent—the pursuit of an enriching life—and as a result are often embittered.
- *Campers* generally work hard, apply themselves, pay their dues, and do what it takes to reach a certain level. Then they plant their tent stakes and settle down at their current elevation.
- *Climbers* are the rare breed who continue to learn, grow, strive, and improve until their final breath, who look back at life and say: "I gave it my all."

It's no coincidence that Climbers are the people we most admire, and are drawn to, and seek to become. One of the major discoveries of my research is that the heart of the difference between Climbers and Campers or Quitters is what they do with adversity.

Relentlessly pursuing a life, or building an organization, rich in purpose can be pretty tough. The weather on the mountain is intense. That's why Quitters abandon the ascent and Campers hunker down. Only Climbers take on the immensely gratifying challenge of learning, striving, improving, and contributing until their final breath.

According to our poll of 150,000 leaders across all industries worldwide, many people quit (5 to 20 percent), most camp (65 to 90 percent), and a rare few climb. In fact, when leaders were asked, "What percentage of your workforce is camping?" the most common response was "80 percent."

This is a *tragic* loss of potential, at a time when the price of camping is increasingly costly, and the benefits of climbing are particularly rich. But my previous books stopped short of explaining something powerfully distinct about Climbers. I have discovered that the people with the highest AQs don't simply respond more effectively to adversity. Whether they are driving a new business model, forging an exceptional team, or simply finding ways to accelerate their own development, they *use* adversity. And in this process, they unleash tremendous energy and innovation, and gain momentum. This book will teach you how to use your adversities—not necessarily catastrophes, but setbacks, disappointments, and difficulties—to unleash your personal best.

My research led me to Erik Weihenmayer because he is a Climber in the truest sense of the word. He attacks life as he attacks a rock face—with a relentless determination to elevate himself and everyone around him—whether through his stirring narratives as a keynote speaker, his groundbreaking and highly visible adventures, or his outreach to marginalized people throughout the world. Climbers strive to improve themselves and their worlds. With regard to anything that matters, phrases like *almost, at least we tried,* or *there's no way* are words outside Erik's vocabulary. The words that are true to his character are *more, better, smarter, faster, richer,* and *higher.*

In short, Erik is the living embodiment of every lesson offered in this book. Erik is the true exemplar of *The Adversity Advantage.* In this book, I will help decode Erik's emotional DNA so that you can infuse his inner tenacity and greatness into your own life. Erik will provide you with his best, terrain-tested wisdom and insights, using spellbinding stories to help you fundamentally rethink and retool your relationship with adversity.

The Seven Summits of Adversity

After teaching people about the power of adversity in business and in life for the past twenty-five years, I know that everyone can learn the practical tools for harnessing adversity as a vital life force. The new principles and practices offered in this book are not crafted for superheroes or impossible extremes. They are devised for us normal folks so that we can begin to achieve everyday greatness in our own day-to-day lives.

Summit One: Take It On! defines in a simple, practical way the adversities you face. You will learn how you, those around you, and even your organization can Take It On—get past the frustration, helplessness, anger, and even acceptance of adversity and reach the point where you can embrace and benefit from its force. You'll learn why you are better equipped for the big adversities than you are for the everyday onslaught of energy-draining annoyances. You will begin to get a sense of how adversity can be both the ultimate competitive weapon for a business, and the ultimate fuel for a life. You will learn where you currently reside on the Adversity Continuum—the ultimate gauge of your relationship with life's tough stuff—so you can begin your journey to higher levels. You will complete your own Adversity Inventory, and emerge with a clearly defined Summit Challenge.

Summit Two: Summon Your Strengths challenges the conventional wisdom that natural strengths are the driving force of success. This chapter will help you recognize your natural strengths, decide what skills you want to develop, and determine what you need from others to achieve your Summit Challenge. You will develop your Adversity Strengths through the powerful combination of courage, discipline, and tenacity. You will break through your notions of what you and others can or should attempt to do. You will rethink how you team up with others in business and in life.

Summit Three: Engage Your CORE discusses how to handle every adversity better and faster. You will gain vital insight into the four CORE dimensions—Control, Ownership, Reach, and Endurance—that determine how people respond to adversity. You will devise your own personal CORE Strategy for moving up the Adversity Continuum to begin turning specific adversities into real advantage.

Summit Four: Pioneer Possibilities is about devising your personal Signature Systems for making the impossible, possible. You will create unique strategies that others have simply failed to devise. Learn how you and your organization can gain tremendous traction and momentum through the force of adversity. You will rethink how you approach limitations, as well as expand your perception of what's possible. You will learn to shift from "what now?" to "what if?"

Summit Five: Pack Light, Pack Right includes lessons from Erik's vivid world of climbing. There are many kinds of baggage, both emotional and tangible. Packing poorly will cripple you, but carefully choosing the right things, people, obligations, and pursuits will *strengthen* you. The more weighed down you are, or your organization is, the less agile and effective you are when attacking adversity. Kill agility, and you suffocate alchemy. In this chapter you will gain the clarity to spring-clean your life so you can rise up, rather than crumble under the weight of each new adversity.

Summit Six: Suffer Well introduces the concept of productive suffering. No matter how fortunate you may be, you will eventually be given the opportunity to suffer. So the question is, will you suffer poorly or well? Adversity Alchemists have the amazing capacity to suffer well—to elevate those around them through their own losses and hardships. They turn pain into beauty. Suffering can be tragic, debilitating, and stultifying, or it can be high-octane fuel for accelerated alchemy. Potent reactions usually involve heat. That's why character is forged in the flames of adversity. Done right, suffering can fuel greatness.

Summit Seven: Deliver Greatness, Every Day is the culmination of the preceding six summits. It brings together the most important ideas from the entire book, providing a coherent, portable package of practices you can take with you and apply anywhere, anytime, so you can rise to the very top of the Adversity Continuum. You will be able to perform your own brand of alchemy. Life's lead becomes gold, darkness becomes light, and normality turns into greatness. And you will emerge poised, if not anxious, for the advantage you will gain from each new adversity.

The Mountain Metaphor

Erik and I have chosen the mountain as our metaphor, not to represent a testosterone-induced, tackle-the-summit athletic feat, but as a universal symbol of inspiration and aspiration. People share a drive to ascend—to move forward and upward in our lives; to gain, rather than lose, elevation. Don't worry. You certainly don't have to be a climber or an athlete to relate to all this. So while Erik's stories from the world's higher peaks may sound impossibly daunting, the lessons within those stories link quite practically to the more normal, often involuntary challenges and hardships we all face in the course of our various endeavors.

Erik

Life Is Not Fair. Next?

To be blunt, adversity is utterly heartless. It is completely indifferent to our success or failure. It doesn't care about our human definition of fairness or justice, and it would just as soon crush us as propel us through its gauntlet. Like a gale-force wind, it can do serious damage. Or, if harnessed, it can take you farther than you could otherwise go. The exciting news is that no matter how mundane or irritating your hassles may be, they can be used for dramatic gains. And it all begins with Summit One, when you turn into the storm and Take It On!

Moving toward the summit of Denali on our nineteenth day, we still had a mile and most of the steep climbing to go.

Take It On!

MOUNT MCKINLEY (DENALI)

Base Camp: 7,200 feet
Summit: 20,320 feet
Located in Alaska, Mount McKinley is the tallest peak in North America.

Kites rise highest against the wind; not with it.

–SIR WINSTON CHURCHILL

ROUTE DESCRIPTION

► Adversity Defined and Scored
  • Inner and Outer Adversity . . . Scoring Your Adversity
► Why Look for Adversity?
  • Cloud Seeding . . . The Big Stuff versus the Small Stuff
► The Adversity Continuum
  • Stage 1: Avoiding Adversity
  • Stage 2: Surviving Adversity
  • Stage 3: Coping with Adversity
  • Stage 4: Managing Adversity
  • Stage 5: Harnessing Adversity
► Your Adversity Assumptions

- ▸ Your Adversity Inventory
  - • Step 1: Categorize Your Life
  - • Step 2: Declare Your Aspirations
  - • Step 3: Prioritize Your Pain
  - • Step 4: Pick Your Adversities
  - • Step 5: Pinpoint Your Summit Challenge
  - • Step 6: Select Your Summit Adversity
  - • Step 7: Clear the Trail
- ▸ Turn into the Storm
- ▸ Sometimes Attitude Corrections Are Forced upon Us
- ▸ Your Take It On! Strategy
- ▸ When Facing the Facts Is Not Enough

Erik

Nobody wakes up hoping for a day filled with adversity. Including me. In fact, I never thought consciously about adversity until it sought me out. Even then, like most people, I did everything in my power to avoid it, downplay it, and deny its existence. Not until I eventually embraced its full force did I begin to understand what I could do and who I could be. And when I look back on the whole process, painful and uncertain as it was, it's hard to imagine my life unfolding in any other way.

The role that adversity plays in our lives was revealed to me in a powerful way on the first of my Seven Summits, Mount McKinley, also called Denali—the highest peak in North America and notorious for its brutal conditions. There I was, a blind guy, wedged into a tent at 7,200 feet. I lay there wondering what stroke of insanity led me ever to believe I could take on a 20,320-foot mountain, let alone one so daunting. I slid deeper into my sleeping bag, gritting my teeth against the arctic blasts, and remembered how the idea began.

One morning, eighteen months earlier, I had sat at the top of a hundred-foot desert rock pinnacle with my climbing buddy, Sam Bridgham, after a really gratifying climb up a crazy knife-edge arête. We were talking about all the cool routes we had tackled, and Sam remarked on how amazing it was that I could climb at all. Many people told me this, and, frankly, I had grown kind of weary of the accolades. I had nothing against the sincere folks who were affected by my efforts. It moved me to know I influenced their mind-set. No—the fault wasn't theirs; it was mine.

I've always had a restless voice inside me, which seemed to speak loudest when my life felt a bit stagnant. Stepping into new and challenging situations often created positive results for me. I remember during my freshman year of high school, tapping my white cane down an empty hallway toward the wrestling room, to try a sport I had a hunch blind people could do. A few years later, I tried rock climbing because it sounded crazy but just maybe I could do it. And after college, I moved alone across the country, from New England to the southwestern desert, a place I knew nothing about, to start a life as a middle school teacher. I think we all have that voice inside us, haunting us in a good way, if we will only listen. Thank God for that voice. We'd never grow without it.

When I was an English teacher, my students and I were reading one of my favorite short stories, "The Secret Life of Walter Mitty," by James Thurber. I felt a lot like Walter. He definitely has that little voice egging him on to do something great with his life. He imagines himself facing all sorts of adverse situations. First he is captain of a U.S. Navy hydroplane in the middle of a horrific storm, then a famous surgeon performing a life-saving operation, and then a bomber pilot in the Royal Air Force flying a secret wartime mission over Germany. But we learn, sadly, that Walter's brave adventures are only daydreams.

For me, that little voice was getting louder and louder. I guess I longed for more than daydreams. At age twenty-five, I had already gained a lot of attention as "the blind rock climber," and I knew that if I just kept pursuing the same level of challenges, no one would ever accuse me of being a slacker. Blindness could have been my ticket to cruising on autopilot, the bar set at the current level and thus relieving me from ever having to stretch or face any further self-imposed hardships.

So, on top of that desert rock face, when Sam asked me, "What do you say we try something a little bigger?" I was definitely intimidated. "I'm thinking about McKinley," he continued, and then began explaining all about this massive peak in Alaska. "That's a *lot* bigger!" is all I could say, and I laughed nervously. As Sam spoke, I began to understand that his proposal would involve immense pain, relentless training, and enormous adversity—with great odds of failing. I also sensed, though, with a gut-wrenching blend of excitement and dread, that I was headed to Mount McKinley. I loved climbing, but even more important, I burned to take on the impossible and, in the process, elevate my own life and maybe even the lives of others.

It may sound crazy, a blind novice taking on such a dangerous mountain; but in many ways McKinley was the perfect big peak on which to begin. Since all of the route is glaciated, crisscrossed by giant gaping crevasses, the only way to climb it is to be roped up with teammates. Even when the wind was howling and I wouldn't be able to hear footsteps crunching in front of me, I'd have the direction of the rope to follow. Also, although McKinley is steep, its snowy surface is generally smooth, so most of my steps would be relatively consistent.

I eagerly plunged into all the preparations. There was so much for me to learn: how to throw myself down on my ice axe in case a teammate slipped into a crevasse; how to pull the teammate out with a pulley and rope; how to put up tents while wearing thick gloves; and how to cook freeze-dried meals on a camp stove by touch. I even read in Braille a stack of accident reports, with the crystal-clear goal of *not* becoming McKinley's 199th recorded fatality. I saw each new obstacle as a way of fully confronting difficult issues before they had a chance to defeat us.

Finally the day arrived when Cessna planes, packed to the ceilings with gear, flew our team across the Alaska Range, their skis skidding onto the ice runway at Base Camp. From that point, day after day, we lugged sixty-pound packs and pulled fifty-pound sleds up the glacier, often sinking in snow up to our knees and pushing through howling blizzards. The days just kept getting harder.

Two weeks into the trip, as I kicked steps up a steep headwall, my colossal pack felt like it was compressing my spine and mashing my internal organs. The strap around my chest was suffocating me as I gasped in the oxygen-poor air, and with each exhausting step I'd gain a foot, only to slide back two feet. On a downhill hike, after dropping off a load of gear at a higher camp, I found myself constantly sliding into the deep boot holes frozen in the trail; my ankles and being wrenched at bizarre angles. I staggered back into our camp at 14,500 feet and lay in the snow outside my tent, utterly spent. I was dizzy and nauseated, puking in the snow, tears welling up in my eyes. I honestly wasn't sure whether I had what it took to wake up the next morning and do it all over again.

Every day became a new education on just how far I could push myself. I struggled physically, and, most of all, mentally. But nineteen days after flying in, we reached the summit, a little lump of snow in the sky. We learned later it was Helen Keller's birthday.

When we got down to Base Camp, my wife, Ellen, who had flown in to meet us, said I looked like a hunched-over old man. My face was scaly with windburn on top of sunburn. Afterward, a reporter asked me what I was going to climb next. I told him I was going to climb into bed for a long nap. Physically I was trashed, but inwardly something had changed. It was as though an internal reservoir of energy and purpose, which should have been completely dry, had actually grown fuller. My mind and spirit burned with a boundless vitality I hadn't known I possessed.

Then, unexpectedly, the letters and cards began to pour in. There were bundles of them, and some were in Braille. They came from classrooms and families all over the world, as far away as India and Japan. Many were from parents whose blind children were struggling to hang on to hope. This entire adventure had begun with a small voice inside my head urging me on. Now that voice was being joined by a chorus of blind children and their parents, and they were telling me to climb higher. It was then I began to dream of the Seven Summits.

At 16,000 feet on Denali, my team members and I pause at a huge precipice at the top of the headwall. Sam Bridgham described for me the view looking across to Mount Foraker and 10,000 feet down to our Base Camp on the Kahiltna Glacier and a giant crevasse we had crossed weeks ago.

I never set out to climb a mountain as a way of breaking records or becoming anyone's hero; but, probably like you, I've wanted to breathe in as much joy, fulfillment, and accomplishment as humanly possible. Despite our fears and our perceived limitations, we don't have to remain Walter Mittys, always dreaming with a hollow feeling inside. No matter how big our adversities may be, if we turn into the storm, we expand the impact and richness of our lives.

Paul

Adversity Defined and Scored

Adversity happens. It doesn't play favorites, and it comes in all shapes and sizes. And your natural response might be "Take It Away!" rather than "Take It On!"

People are endlessly resourceful. Serious adversity often leads to a triumph of human spirit and ingenuity. In enterprise, the greatest inventions and advancements are created in response to adversity. But what about your everyday adversities? Someone drops the ball on an important project, leaving you hanging out to dry. Your e-mail crashes. The platters for the party weren't delivered to your client in time. Your son's teacher just called you at work about "his recent behavior." You get sick when you can least afford it. Someone you love is down-and-out. Your classes got dropped. Your car's engine light goes on at the worst possible time. These are everyday events, or perhaps they all happen on the *same* day. The truth is that adversity is a part of most days. Whether you are ultimately weakened or strengthened by each event, or the accumulation of events, will depend on you first mastering the ability to Take It On!

Defining adversity is the first step. What exactly are you supposed to take on? What exactly *is* adversity to you? Adversity is *personal, relative*, and *universal*.

Inner and Outer Adversity

It may be useful to categorize adversity into two areas: 1) *Inner Adversity* (internal physical, mental, emotional, and spiritual states that cause you hardship), and 2) *Outer Adversity* (things that occur externally that cause you difficulty). We all have varying degrees of both. In whatever manner, everyone, including you, faces life's tough stuff.

Most people think of adversity only as something serious or terrible. But it really encompasses the entire range of hassles, obstacles, difficulties, hardships, misfortune, setbacks, and challenges, even those we willingly take on ourselves. For the purposes of this book, we will go by this powerful yet simple definition:

Adversity is something that has a negative impact, or is predicted to have a negative impact, on someone or something you care about.

EXAMPLES OF INNER ADVERSITY

• Lack of confidence	• Depression	• Self-doubt
• Lethargy	• Self-loathing	• Fatigue
• Fear, anxiety	• Physical pain	• Poor health
• Uncertainty	• Loneliness	• Insomnia

EXAMPLES OF OUTER ADVERSITY

• Someone violates your trust	• You receive a serious diagnosis
• You experience a natural disaster	• Your coworker is out to get you
• All flights are canceled	• You fail a class
• There is an economic downturn	• Your insurance rates double
• Your best friend moves away	• A loved one passes away
• Your computer dies	• A noisy neighbor moves in next door

Scoring Your Adversity

Sometimes it is difficult to distinguish adversity from annoyance, especially since one person's annoyance (a scratch on the new car) could be another person's catastrophe. People often disagree—even argue vehemently—about how serious a given adversity may be. One person might see an event as minor, while another perceives it as utterly devastating.

How you experience adversity is determined by 1) its *impact*—the real or imagined, existing or potential severity, and 2) its *importance*—how much it matters to you. For your own clarity, and to reach clarity with others, use the simple exercise of scoring the magnitude of any adversity. This gives you something firm for comparison, since adversity is all relative.

If an event has an impact on something that matters greatly to you, with a potentially disastrous effect, then you might score that adversity as nine on a ten-point scale. If something minor happens to something you barely care about, you might score that adversity as a two. If you have been saving for your golden years and there is a stock market crash just before your retirement, you might rate this event an eight or nine. On the other hand, if you have only a few minor investments, you might rate the same event a five.

Scoring adversity this way can ease some common conflicts between partners, colleagues, and teammates. If a given event scores as ten for you and as three for your colleague, that would explain why you are much more intense and urgent about that issue. If someone appears to be overly ramped up over an issue you consider minor, it's likely that he or she scores the adversity higher than you do. If an event significantly affects someone important to you—such as your boss—it now, by definition, becomes an adversity for you. If your customer is going ballistic over a "silly thing," and you are not, chances are there's a scoring discrepancy. Try asking this: "To help me understand where you're coming from, on a scale of one to ten, if ten is as bad as it can get, and one is nothing, how would you rate this situation?" Getting to the heart of the matter—*why* your adversity scores are so far apart—can lead to real resolution and results.

Other people's scores, just like your own, may be dramatically influenced by past experience. People who experienced their ten on the front lines of war or as victims of violent crime may rate nothing else higher than a six or seven for the rest of their lives. But others who have faced little adversity might consider a long line at their favorite restaurant a most distressing setback. You might find it difficult not to judge this behavior as "spoiled," but it's all relative.

For a long time it had seemed to me that life was about to begin—real life.
But there was always some obstacle in the way, something to be gotten through
first, some unfinished business, time still to be served, a debt to be paid.
Then life would begin.
At last it dawned on me that these obstacles were my life.
—ALFRED D. SOUZA

Why Look for Adversity?

Scoring your adversity is one thing. What about those people you know who seem to seek or create adversity? Some people live for drama. I call them "emotional storm chasers."

The Discovery Channel on television has a show called *Storm Chasers*, highlighting escapees from the asylum of common sense who somehow reached the conclusion that the best use of their vacations would be to track tornadoes or to hurl themselves into hurricanes. The program usually showcases some lightning-fueled zealot racing across the American prairies, trying to catch the best-ever footage of a cyclone by anyone whose car is not suddenly tossed into a neighboring state. These people get their buzz from adverse weather. The worse it is, and the closer they get, the faster their veins pulse, and the higher their voices squeal.

The purpose of this book is *not* to turn you into an emotional storm chaser. In most cases, the weather will find you, wherever you are. And, there is nothing you can do to change it. On the other hand, as the saying goes, when you are given a lemon . . . make lemonade.

Cloud Seeding

If your life is a little too calm and predictable, then you may wish to do some *cloud seeding* to stir up your skies. I regularly coach organizational leaders to do this, to awaken their people's inner strengths and unleash their higher potential. Cloud seeding usually involves picking the right clouds—that is, the right issues—to mess with. These are the ones you think may yield the greatest results. Given the calm that may come from a successful year or a winning streak, you may wish to stir up some adversity at work by confronting the one issue that is holding things back and preventing the achievement of the next level of success. Socially, you may decide to confront that friend who is living in denial or for whom a wake-up call may offer enormous potential benefit. Or you may seek to work through a festering misunderstanding that could renew your relationship with someone important. Personally, you may decide to take on some chronic shortcoming to open up new possibilities. What clouds might you seed to help you reach your goals?

The Big Stuff versus the Small Stuff

I have to address a reaction you may be having after reading Erik's story at the opening of this chapter. Sometimes when we hear these amazing tales of people who face the really big stuff and do extraordinary things, it's hard to relate. Our adversities may seem so small in comparison that we don't even think their example may apply to us, so we think, "They're different." Quite the contrary. The truth is that you can learn to perform the same sort of alchemy with your adversities as Erik did with his.

Have you noticed that you respond to some adversities more effectively than to others? It turns out that taking on the small problems can actually be tougher than taking on the big ones. In our *Adversity Advantage* programs we have had countless people come up to us perplexed. They usually say something like "I just don't get it. When my teenager was in a car accident, I was incredibly strong. But my computer crashing can just debilitate me! Why is that?"

There is a reason why people are often more effective at taking on the big setbacks. You are constructed, through the fierce power of the flight-fight response, to draw forth previously unknown powers when big trouble hits. Earthquake? Tornado? Plane crash? You can rally. A flush of adrenaline fortifies you for fast and powerful action. But what about a slow, constant drizzle? Or a gray, overcast chill? It turns out that we humans do not have a similar protective mechanism for bringing out our best in these less dramatic conditions. We are more naturally equipped to respond to the big stuff. But we can deliberately install the mechanism we need for optimizing the small stuff, too. We can shine forth in gray weather by mastering the Seven Summits offered in this book.

The Adversity Continuum

The Adversity Continuum describes, in ascending order, five different ways of dealing with setbacks and disappointments. In this section, you will learn how, by ascending further up the Adversity

Continuum, you can increase your energy, along with your everyday greatness.

> *This is the true joy in life . . . being used for a purpose recognized by*
> *yourself as a mighty one . . . being thoroughly worn out before you*
> *are thrown on the scrap heap . . . being a force of Nature instead of*
> *a feverish selfish little clod of ailments and grievances complaining*
> *that the world will not devote itself to making you happy.*
> —GEORGE BERNARD SHAW

From your own experience you know there are at least two kinds of fatigue. Over the course of your day, year, and life, you can be used up in a *good* way, or you can be used up in a *bad* way. Being used up in a good way means pouring forth your finest effort toward an engaging, elevating cause. Being used up in a bad way happens when you expend your precious life force being pummeled by adversity, suffering real loss, with little if any gain.

In our research, the vast majority of folks (87 percent of more than 150,000 respondents) reported that, more often than not, they were fatigued in a bad way. They felt drained by adversity, and the only relief they could imagine was the fantasy of an adversity-free life, such as a perfect vacation or blissful retirement. The problem is that there is no such thing as an "adversity-free" life. The solution is to learn how to live the life you've got, adversity and all.

Adversity *can* sap your life force. But it doesn't *have* to. Why spend your best effort fighting the very wind that can fill your sails and take you to otherwise unreachable lands?

> *I firmly believe that any man's finest hour, his greatest fulfillment*
> *to all he holds dear, is the moment he has worked his heart out in a*
> *good cause and lies exhausted on the field of battle victorious.*
> —VINCE LOMBARDI

The Adversity Continuum depicts the range of our approaches to life's tough stuff. It is a steep climb that few complete. As with most mountains, it is at the lower elevations where you find the crowds. But the higher you go, the better it gets.

We need to rethink our relationship with and assumptions about adversity . . . and life. People who glean the greatest advantage from their adversities learn to Take It On!

Stage 1: Avoiding Adversity

At the bottom of the continuum resides one of our most natural and instinctive responses to any adversity—*avoiding it*. And a classic avoidance mechanism is *denial*. While denial spares you pain and can buy you time, it prevents you from taking on adversity. As a result, the potential benefit that adversity might bring is delayed, or even denied to you.

Avoiding and denying adversity can be exhausting, like endlessly hiking the entire way around the base of a mountain, rather than taking it on. People who actively try to downplay adversity tend to be haunted by an insidious fear that the thing they're working so hard to avoid will forever remain, or worse yet, mutate, come back to life, and strike again.

Avoiding adversity can create cancerous emotions like self-doubt and even self-loathing. A morbidly obese man who wakes up each day fully aware that he needs to lose weight, and who is equipped with all the knowledge and tools he needs to actually do so, does not get a boost to his self-esteem with each day he ignores or postpones the hard work it would take to regain his health. So why do people avoid adversity? The benefit comes from preserving an easier, more comfortable state. It's often a lot easier—at least for the moment—to stay where you are than to climb to a better place.

Avoidance is unique. It is based not on what you do, but on what you choose *not* to do. A sure sign that you are avoiding adversity is feeling sapped not by something you experienced, but by something you chose *not* to experience. If you've ever spent considerable effort escaping a situation you may have been dreading, then you know that, ironically, the energy you expend avoiding an adversity may ultimately exceed the energy required to Take It On!

Denial has its place. Temporarily, it can protect you from total despair. And avoidance can be useful if it helps you set the priorities that allow you to get moving. When the onslaught of adversities is potentially overwhelming, you may strategically decide which hardships to sidestep, and which ones to take on.

Erik went through this stage in his young life as he was going blind. Many know Erik as the amazing blind guy who climbed Everest and the Seven Summits, but his relationship with adversity has been more complex than a sound bite can ever capture. When he was a boy, his fear and dread of going blind were so overwhelming that he just could not accept this adversity, let alone Take It On. That's the real story, which he explains vividly below.

Erik

Short-Term Denial versus Long-Term Delusion

Denial protected me from both pain and possibility. Even as I was slowly losing my sight, week by week, bit by bit, the idea of total blindness loomed like some vague nightmare way out there in the future. Amazingly, I was able to convince myself that it wasn't happening. I had placed myself in a state of suspended animation, unable to go forward, unable to go back, trapped in an isolated cell of complete stagnation. Doctors had clearly told me and my family that I'd be blind by my early teens, but, although this may be hard to believe, I convinced myself that their diagnosis had been a mistake, that there were other reasons why I couldn't see as well as I had the day before. I had an explanation for everything: "The sun is right in my eyes. The lighting in this room is terrible. Words look smaller in books because publishers are squeezing more words onto the page to save money." When something happened so overwhelmingly clear that I couldn't explain it away, contemplating the prospect of blindness was so frightening that I'd pull away from the thought, blocking it off as if slamming a prison door shut.

Some have told me that my brain's brilliant con job seems almost ridiculous. How could you have turned away from the obvious facts of the situation? My answer is simple: the mind is enormously powerful. No matter what the facts, no matter what the overwhelming evidence, it has a remarkable capacity to convince us of whatever we want to believe.

If this sounds unlikely, consider the alcoholic who is unable to see his dependency despite the devastating effect it has on his life and family. Or consider the chronically poor performer who is genuinely shocked when he gets fired, even after many serious discussions about his work. So surprisingly, when I woke up one morning just before my freshman year in high school, completely blind, it came as a massive blow for which I was totally unprepared.

Paul

Stage 2: Surviving Adversity

Likewise, *surviving* adversity can be downright arduous—the goal being simply to come through still standing, or at least alive. Sometimes, given dismal enough circumstances, survival is exceptionally noble, even inspiring, and is all one can hope for, at least temporarily. Hanging on tenaciously for another day without food or water while pinned under earthquake rubble is elevating behavior. Slogging off to a job you hate, day after day, year after year, just because it's easier than bettering your circumstances, is not.

With avoidance you go around; with survival you go through. With survival you often experience completion. With avoidance you do not. Ideally, survival is only a temporary stopping point on the way to higher elevations. Like avoidance, being stuck in survival mode tends to be intensely draining, because you invest enormous energy, and you gain little if any ground. The longer it lasts, the tougher this stage gets. Most people are not at their best when in survival mode. They desperately lash out in an effort to preserve themselves, often at the expense of others. If your motto is "Every day aboveground is a good one," you are probably spending too much time in survival mode.

Stage 3: Coping with Adversity

Constructive coping begins with acceptance. Drinking yourself into oblivion is not a good coping mechanism. If you are still making attempts to flee from your adversity, or trying to blame it on someone else, you are not at the coping stage.

Coping is one step up from surviving because you are taking constructive steps to define the nature of your adversity, to coexist with it as best you can, and to protect your well-being. When you are coping with adversity, it helps to talk to friends, get some fresh air, take a long run, or do some other kind of physical exercise that will help reduce the stress that comes with recognizing your predicament. Erik coped with total blindness by telling himself that he'd simply have to navigate the best he could despite his diminished abilities and expectations.

Adversity deserves whatever time and energy are required to glean the fullest possible benefit. Many people get stuck in coping mode because the perceived impact of the adversity is so great that it takes all they have just to stay even or prevent a downslide. The problem arises when you expend tremendous resources coping with adversity but do not gain any ground. You'll get by, but over time you'll experience more detriment than advantage. The best you can hope for at this stage is restoring yourself to your earlier form. You might emerge unscathed, but you've lost precious time, energy, and opportunity in the process.

![Erik]

Just Getting By

I coped with going blind by telling myself that, although I'd never be the same, I'd just have to live with it—as a person lives with a debilitating disease. I begrudgingly took the long white cane that the professionals gave me and went through the motions, but I still felt helpless, unable to affect the direction of my life, like a dried leaf blowing in a storm. Wherever I'd land, I'd try to react, usually badly and often with visceral anger. My response was primitive, like a cornered badger baring his teeth and lashing out at the world.

I tried to accept the fact that I could no longer do many of the things I loved: riding my bike, watching movies, and horsing around with friends. I was coping as best I could, but some days I'd sit in the cafeteria listening to the excitement, laughter, and food fights passing me by, and I'd see my life through a rearview mirror, looking into the past, looking at all the things I once could do and had lost. I wasn't afraid of going blind and seeing darkness, but I was terrified of being swept to the sidelines, afraid that at the ripe old age of fourteen I'd be a nonfactor, unimportant, and forgotten. My hopes for the future had been snatched away. By coping, I was barely keeping my head above water, but I was still slowly drowning.

Paul

Stage 4: Managing Adversity

Managing adversity requires being actively engaged with it. When you manage adversity, you are trying to contain it, and to minimize its downside and its potential impact on other facets of your life or organization. Sometimes just managing adversity becomes a full-time job.

We've been raised to believe that effective leaders and individuals manage adversity well. Managing adversity is like operating a moderately effective furnace. It's more productive than avoiding, surviving, or coping, but it uses substantial energy and does not unleash adversity's full potential.

When you work to affect your adversity in some positive way, you are managing it. Done right, managing adversity can be an effective way to keep it in check. People with chronic pain and illness often learn to manage their adversity in elevating ways, whether they are eventually cured or not. When Erik uses a talking computer, a guide dog, or a Braille writer, he is managing his adversity by working with it more effectively. But whether for Erik or for you, everyday greatness requires moving up the Adversity Continuum to a higher level of engagement.

Stage 5: Harnessing Adversity

When you use adversity to elevate yourself and others, or for some tangible gain, that's *harnessing* adversity. When you are living at the lower levels of the Adversity Continuum, you are consuming your life force and losing energy. It is only at the level of *harnessing* your adversity that your "furnace" produces more energy than it uses. Living at the top of the Adversity Continuum gives you a big energy boost, as well as a boost of confidence. It drives innovation, builds momentum, and strengthens your morale. By using adversity to your advantage, you can accelerate your progress toward an important goal, create competitive gains, and produce fuel for your dreams.

Most of us spend time moving between the levels of the Adversity Continuum. It's not like we can flick a switch or swallow a magic pill and suddenly become impervious to tragedy. The key is to minimize the time we spend in the lower levels, and maximize the time spent at the top.

Whenever you face something exceptionally tough, it's only natural to bemoan all that may be lost. It is much tougher to ponder, and then pursue, what can be potentially *gained*.

Your Adversity Assumptions

Erik inspires us with his example of how one person, even with initial reluctance, can transform his relationship with adversity. But to do so, he had to come to grips with his underlying Adversity Assumptions: that blindness would make him obsolete, and that denying it would make it go away.

Adversity can provide the challenge, the kick in the pants, that helps you grow. Most people's Adversity Assumptions run along the lines of "less is more." Ask them what they think about adversity, and they may say something like "I have enough trouble! I have money problems, marriage problems, even medical problems. Come to think of it, I need a drink!"

Overall, "less adversity is better" drives much of our financial planning equation, and many of our choices about how we live. Many of us think that an ideal life would be simpler, calmer, more predictable, and easier. We build gated communities where we attempt to keep chaos out and calm predictability within. We take vacations to get away from our hassles, if only for a few days. Parents do all they can to reduce their children's adversity instead of allowing them to contend with some adversity on their own.

Check your own assumptions. Do you agree with the premise that we can gain some advantage from our difficulties if we use them properly? Most of the time, people miss the opportunity to gain real advantage when adversity strikes because they have negative underlying assumptions about hardship.

I worked with a client recently to unearth his deeper Adversity Assumptions. In his own words, they included:

1. "It is *my* job to shoulder it, and to protect my loved ones from adversity."
2. " 'Success' can be gauged by how effectively you eliminate adversity from your life."

Now think about your own Adversity Assumptions. What would the people who see you most and know you best guess your assumptions about adversity to be? How have you handled adversity in the past? Do you think it would be possible for you to think creatively about setbacks and disappointments? Are you able to see adversity in a positive light? When trouble is on the horizon, do you want to run and hide, or do you recognize that by engaging with adversity you will have an opportunity to learn and to grow?

When adversity finds you, it's human nature to ask, "Why me?" People who have mastered living at the top of the Adversity Continuum say, "Why not me?" and go on to find a way to turn their challenges into victories. Adversity is not only potentially good, but *essential* for everyday greatness.

Your Adversity Inventory

It takes courage to do a full inventory of your adversities. But all worthy ascents begin with a process of coming to grips with where you are, so you can move ahead. In this section, you will learn how to complete your own Adversity Inventory to help you pinpoint two things:

1. *Your Summit Challenge.* This is the one accomplishment you have always wanted to do.
2. *Your Summit Adversity.* This is the one setback that offers you the greatest potential power, if harnessed.

You will be using your Summit Challenge and Summit Adversity throughout this book, and beyond. Two sample Adversity Inventories, one for a college student I will call Tanya, and one for Erik, are provided at the end of this section to help you think through your own circumstances.

This exercise is all about making it to the top of the Adversity Continuum. If you are still at the bottom level, Avoiding Adversity, you will need to get out of denial before you can begin assessing your adversities. If you are Surviving Adversity, you are not in a position—yet—to start sorting through the lesser adversities in your life. If you are Coping with Adversity, you may get stuck at that level if you think it's the best you can do, or you may step up to Managing Adversity, where you begin to make a positive impact on your circumstances. Use this section to make the transition to Harnessing Adversity, where you release the good that is hidden inside a problem or setback that, on the surface, looks pretty bad.

Step 1: Categorize Your Life

Across the top of a page, list all the categories of life that matter to you, including family, work, friends, community, health, hobbies, and so on. Write down headings that cover all your interests and obligations. Then double-check your categories. It is amazing how easily we can let something significant temporarily slip out of our consciousness. In a recent program of ours, a stressed-out corporate manager and mother of three forgot the category "children," even though she remembered to list her leadership position in her condominium association. Her head was in "professional mode" and it took her several moments to take in the full panorama of her life.

Step 2: Declare Your Aspirations

List your top two or three aspirations for each category of your life. These are things you have not yet accomplished, but which you aspire to achieve, short or long term. If you have a specific goal ("learn to play guitar"), try to determine the underlying aspiration that is really motivating you ("reconnect with my natural interests and abilities that got lost as I got older"). If your goal is a negative ("not go bankrupt"), put it in positive terms so you have something to achieve ("avoid bankruptcy and get accounts in the black again"). If you are sick, your number-one goal may be "not die." See if you can turn that into "live well and love well, for as long as I can"—a worthy goal for all of us.

Step 3: Prioritize Your Pain

Thoughtfully consider and then list the top two or three adversities that are causing you the most pain or discomfort within each category. This is your chance to think about the different kinds of adversities that are using up your energy and standing in the way between you and your aspirations.

Again, look for the underlying truth. Your initial thought may not reveal the true pain source. We often cite the symptom rather than the cause. Think about the pain beneath the pain, and enter *that* on your list. For example, Tanya recognizes that she has procrastinated about changing her major. Putting things off creates problems, so feeling bad about procrastinating is on her Prioritize Your Pain list ("I'm ashamed I let this go on so long"). However, Tanya's procrastination is a sign of a deeper problem: the fear of letting down her parents if she changes majors and has to stay in school longer before she can graduate. Usually the pain beneath the pain is a fear—in Tanya's case, the fear of upsetting her parents—and much of the time what we fear most is loss.

Double-check your depth and honesty. Did you get to the pain beneath the pain? As long as pain remains unrecognized, you are stuck on avoidance, the bottom stage of the Adversity Continuum.

Step 4: Sort Your Adversities

Scrutinize the adversities you listed in Step 3 and pick one from each category that, if you took it on, would unleash the greatest amount of energy in your life. Did you pick the easiest or the most important? Did you pick the one most important to others, or to you? Go for heft. Being bigger, tougher, and deeper, these adversities carry more force. Remember, the tougher the adversity, the richer the ore to perform your alchemy.

Step 5: Pinpoint Your Summit Challenge

Let's rise above your various aspirations to your overarching Summit Challenge. What percolates inside you when you ponder the word *challenge*? Does it induce trepidation or make you sit up a little straighter? Does it turn your gut in knots or infuse you with determination? The dictionary defines *challenge* as "a situation that tests somebody's abilities in a stimulating way." I might add, "and that includes a certain dose of adversity along the way."

You will want to make sure your Summit Challenge is stated in a way that:

- *Excites*, maybe even frightens you
- *Enriches* you deeply
- *Inspires* your strongest will
- *Connects* to your highest "why"
- *Improves* you—makes you better
- *Benefits others* (ultimately) in some meaningful way, if successful
- *Builds capacity*—demonstrates and strengthens your capacity for future challenges
- *Fuels greatness*—demonstrates and strengthens your everyday greatness

So, Step 5 is to select from your list of aspirations your Summit Challenge: the one most compelling thing you've always wanted to do, but have not yet done (or completed). Write your Summit Challenge at the bottom of your inventory in a way that fits as many of these criteria as possible, since you will work with it throughout the remainder of this book. Erik's Summit Challenge is "to help as many people as possible to strengthen their relationship with adversity."

Step 6: Select Your Summit Adversity

The next step is to select the *one* adversity (obstacle, hardship, difficulty), that 1) you are sure to face as you take on your Summit Challenge, and 2) if harnessed, would offer the greatest potential energy or breakthrough. This is your Summit Adversity. Think of it as a "fuel cell." For decades scientists have been attempting to create free energy—something that generates more energy than it consumes. This is the holy grail of energy research. The true quest is to create a fuel cell that generates greater energy than it expends. Obviously such a discovery could transform society. On a personal level, converting adversity into fuel could transform your life. And this energy source is readily available!

Your Summit Adversity may be the most daunting, most impossible, or most worrisome. Whatever the case, step up and select the one adversity that has the greatest potential upside, once you perform your alchemy. These days Erik's biggest issue has to do with the dynamic tension between his time limitations and the quality he produces, so you'll see on his Adversity Inventory that his Summit Adversity is "finding or making the time to do it right." Insert your own answer at the bottom of your Adversity Inventory.

You may also decide to take all of the challenges you have identified, and thereby make a difference in every aspect of your life, but it's probably easier to focus on one as you learn how to transform adversity into impetus.

Step 7: Clear the Trail

To Take It On! you must unleash the fuel embedded in your Summit Adversity. All that blocks your way is excuses and rationalizations. You must come to grips with the thoughts that prevent you from taking action. With the same courage it took to face the facts, the next step is to take a cold, hard look at what is getting in your way, and to clear the trail of this mental debris.

Excuses sometimes get a bad rap. We tend to label people who make excuses as weak or evasive. But everyone makes excuses, and excuses serve a vital purpose. Excuses are reasons made personal. Excuses are your mechanism for keeping your self-concept— even your *self*—intact, especially when you are under attack. If we confronted you in the hallway and asked you why you are not the number-one, undisputed best in the world at what you do, chances are you have some pretty good reasons. Thankfully, you are not living in a state of soul-crushing anguish over your less-than-best-in-the-world status. That allows you to get on with your life, including your efforts to become even better. That's the upside of excuses.

The obvious downside of excuses is that they become a refuge for doing less than we are capable of doing, often on issues of extreme importance. What are the primary reasons you have *not* harnessed your Summit Adversity so far? Is it because of the extra effort you think it might require? What are the excuses beneath your excuses? What's really at the heart of the matter? For example, "lack of time" is practically a universal excuse. The deeper reason may be fear of discomfort or change.

In general, people are amazingly good at making excuses and rationalizing their shortcomings. Sometimes we would rather

TANYA'S ADVERSITY INVENTORY

		School	Mom's family	Dad's family	Friends	Rowing team	Job at restaurant	Job tutoring
Step 1	Categorize Your Life							
Step 2	Declare Your Aspirations	Graduate on dean's list — Find a way to change to a major I love	Help things around — Create deeper conversation — Find a way to really love each other	Help turn things around — Rejuvenate relationship with Dad — Have one happy holiday	Be lifelong friends with Nikki — Have three real friends	Become captain — Win individual race	Either work up to manager, or get a better job	I should find a way to just quit
Step 3	Prioritize Your Pain	I hate majoring in math — I fear my parents will be upset if I change — I'm ashamed I let this go on so long	Mom's husband treats me like I'm twelve — I hate being a fake big sister	Dad's new girlfriend takes all his time — I hate being in that house	Nikki and I have lost touch — My friends use me for my car	No time to sleep because of practice — Coach is a jerk — We never win	They don't appreciate how hard I work — When other people make mistakes, I pay for it	My heart is not in it — It's too far away — I come unprepared
Step 4	Pick Your Adversities	It's too late to change majors easily	We never talk about things that matter	I hate being at Dad's house	I feel lonely and have no one to talk to	Coach makes it no fun	Not enough recognition at work	Quit tutoring
Step 5	Summit Challenge	Graduate with a degree in a major I actually love, possibly International Affairs						
Step 6	Summit Adversity	I worry that I'm too far along in my studies to change majors						
Step 7	Clear the Trail	Stop worrying about the extra time and money it will take to switch majors. Talk to advisor and find out how to make it work.						

ERIK'S ADVERSITY INVENTORY

		Family	Adventuring	Nonprofit work	Work	Friends	Health
Step 1	Categorize Your Life						
Step 2	Declare Your Aspirations	Spend more time at home Be involved with Emma and Arjun's education	Climb the Eiger Guide twelve injured soldiers up Lobuche Climb K2	No Barriers Expose disabled students to outdoors World Team Sports, take kids climbing Create opportunities for blind kids of the third world	Improve lives and inspire people through adventuring and: Media Writing Films	More outdoor quality time Reconnect with specific folks	Remain injury free Maintain health to enable decades of adventures Do training regimen for two hours every day
Step 3	Prioritize Your Pain	Balancing competing interests Sometimes Ellen worries Missing moments with Emma and Arjun	Insufficient training Endless coordination of details Too much time away from home	Huge time commitment—but it is never enough	Balancing work and training Pressure to stay fresh Knowing when to say no	Never enough time together Drifting apart Separating work from fun	Old injuries, wear and tear Keeping health consistent Finding ways to relax and moments to just be
Step 4	Pick Your Adversities	Ellen's worrying	Overwhelming amount of details	Time commitment	Saving no to worthy offers	Allowing for fun	Relaxation
Step 5	Summit Challenge	To help as many people as possible strengthen their relationship with adversity					
Step 6	Summit Adversity	Finding or making the time to do it right					
Step 7	Clear the Trail	Say no, and help my team say no, to the things that are less "climb-critical"					

deceive ourselves than face the facts, especially if the facts hurt. Similarly, it's far easier to cast blame than to take responsibility. Stepping up to the plate takes courage. If your best friend in the whole world had the ability to see right through you, what would he or she pinpoint as the *real* reason you have not harnessed your adversity so far? Would your friend tell you that you are taking the easy way out?

After giving serious thought to clearing the trail so you can tap into your Summit Adversity, you are ready to hit the road toward your Summit Challenge. Consider what life will be like when you really Take It On!

Turn into the Storm

Although you wouldn't wish blindness on anyone, you may be thinking that in a strange way, Erik was fortunate. Because he could not escape his blindness, he was *forced* to deal with it. And from that mandate, he grew and gained enormously. You may be thinking, "Sure, if I *had* to deal with some tragedy, I would. I'd rise to the challenge, and my heroism would shine through. But it's the daily mundane muck that weighs me down." There is another way.

When you *turn into the storm*, you are consciously deciding to grab the helm and enter the weather, and *not* wait for a wake-up call that forces you into action. It means you confront the full weight of your naked reality, rather than sugarcoating it to make yourself feel better.

Erik

Sometimes Attitude Corrections Are Forced upon Us

I remember the afternoon that I finally decided to turn into the storm. One day, I was walking down a dock near my house, only halfheartedly swinging my cane in front of me, and I accidentally stepped right off the side. I did a flip in the air and landed on my back on the deck of a boat. It was amazing I didn't break my back or crack my head open. I crawled back onto the dock, stunned and terrified. For the first time, my fear of actually dying overwhelmed my hatred of blindness. It didn't matter how much I denied it or avoided it, dreaded it or even hated it. It didn't matter how unfair life was or how much it hurt. No amount of positive attitude was going to help, either. Blindness was real and it had happened. In front of me, I could see two clear paths: In the first, blindness would destroy me; I'd be a ghost, a spectator, listening to life pass me by. In the second, I could squarely face the facts, not as I wished they were or as they ought to be, but as brutal and desperate as they were. I would need to become the ultimate pragmatist and do what it would take to claw my way out.

So I begrudgingly committed to learning how to navigate with my cane and to reading Braille, and the results were surprising. By walking down the hallway using the cane properly, I didn't embarrass myself by bumping into walls and I could actually carry on a conversation with friends. By reading aloud my Brailled essay in class, I felt connected with the other kids. The tools I had loathed for fear they would make me different actually allowed me to reconnect with my classmates and began to bring me back to the world.

I had lived in denial and then tried to cope, because of my overriding assumption that blindness and the techniques that came with it would isolate me and make me feel unfulfilled; but it was only through facing it head-on, even embracing it, that I was able to glimpse the pathway forward.

A few months later, when I got a newsletter about a rock-climbing program for blind kids, I ran my hand up the wall of my room and thought to myself, "Who would be crazy enough to take blind kids rock climbing?" I realized, though, that I couldn't walk with my eyes, but I could use a cane; I couldn't read with my eyes, either, but I could read with my fingers. So I asked myself, what else might be possible if I could gather up the courage to turn into the storm?

If I hadn't fallen off the dock and scared myself into action, I might have gone on merely existing in the lower stages of the Adversity Continuum. But thankfully that scare was the beginning of a long journey toward taking on my adversity, toward fueling a higher level of contribution and a more productive life.

How many of us live in that state of suspended animation? Sometimes adversity permeates the air around us like oppressive moisture before a storm, and we are unable to act. Like some of the people who refuse to evacuate ahead of a hurricane, we squeeze our eyes shut and refuse to look at the dark clouds bearing down on us. Even when we can't help but look, we come up with plausible excuses as to why it is impossible to act. "If I were a little younger, things would be different..." "If others hadn't done those horrible things to me..." "If I had been born taller, smarter, stronger..." Excuses like these are all defense mechanisms to avoid action, barricades summoned up by the mind to protect us from confronting a difficult and painful truth. The only way to really harness the full force of your adversity is to Take It On!

Paul

Your Take It On! Strategy

"Take It On!" is my favorite battle cry for attacking a barrage of adversity. If you know that tough weather is coming, you can drive yourself nuts hoping it doesn't hit, or worrying about what will happen when it does. Or, you can gear up, turn into the onslaught, and say, "Take It On!" The idea, as Erik learned, is to do so not just when you are forced, but proactively, by choice, because it provides the energy you can harness, the lead you can turn to gold.

Earlier you picked your Summit Challenge, the one accomplishment you feel most compelled to do but have never done, and your Summit Adversity, the single most important roadblock that lies between you and the accomplishment of your Summit Challenge. As you read the rest of this book, you will have more than one opportunity to create an action plan for harnessing your Summit Adversity.

Here, just to get started, think through the following questions:

▶ What do you need to do to harness the full force—the full potential—of your Summit Adversity? What actions could you take to unleash the most energy from your situation and cause the most significant positive breakthrough?

▶ What are the benefits you expect to enjoy once you accomplish your Summit Challenge? Be specific, and list them all! Remember to consider all those who, in addition to yourself, will benefit from your success.

▶ What excuses and assumptions do you need to strip away in order to get started?

▶ What courageous conversations do you need to have with others before you start?

▶ When and how will you begin?

▶ Who needs to know?

Tanya, our disenchanted student, wanted to graduate with a degree in a subject she actually loved (her Summit Challenge). She hated her current major (her Summit Adversity). Tanya knew that her personal and professional life would be happier if she focused on a field she enjoyed. She dropped her negative attitude and assumptions about it being too late for her to change majors, and developed an action plan as follows:

Tanya's Action Plan
- ▸ Request an appointment and speak seriously with my advisor about my current concerns. Problem-solve together to come up with possible solutions so I can switch majors.
- ▸ Call the office today, and hope to schedule an appointment by the end of the week.
- ▸ Stop by the Student Financial Services office to discuss the possibility of staying in school for an extra semester, in order to make up the course requirements for my new major.
- ▸ Tell my parents and my roommate.

As so often happens, once Tanya was willing to Take It On, she enjoyed some unexpected advantages. Her conversation with her advisor led to an internship with an international aid agency that Tanya converted into an exciting and meaningful first job upon graduation. If she had not found the courage to *turn into the storm*, Tanya may never have found her path.

Erik

When Facing the Facts Is Not Enough

I have learned from experience that when we *turn into the storm*, the path will almost always get tougher, involve more pain, and take longer than we ever predicted. When it seems the hardest, it will be tremendously tempting to fall back into old habits of denial, coping, and minimizing—those defenses that have failed us time and time again.

Years ago, this happened to me on an attempt of Mount Kenya, a 17,057-foot volcanic rock monolith, jutting vertically out of the East African plains. As always, my climbing partner, Charley Mace, and I prepared diligently, planning our climb for September, smack in the middle of the warm, dry season. We ecstatically envisioned pulling our way up 3,000 feet of finger-width cracks in sunny equatorial Africa, wearing sticky rubber climbing shoes, a helmet, T-shirt, and shorts, in other words, climbers' heaven.

But after a three-day approach in the completely unexpected pouring rain, Charley looked up at the face and was silent for a long time before saying. "E, it's totally different from the pictures. It looks more like a peak in Alaska. The face is covered in snow and ice." His voice revealed astonishment and disappointment. I turned to our local guide. "I thought this was the dry season."

"It is," he insisted, "but with global warming, everything is changing—snowing during dry season—drought during rainy season. The farmers don't even know when to plant their crops anymore."

So our expectations for a quick and pleasant rock climb were dashed. Instead we waited out a week of relentless snowfall, while the face remained shrouded in mist, and hoped the conditions would improve. When it didn't, we sat down to have a frank discussion about our options. The ascent would now become a lot tougher than we had hoped. To have a chance at reaching the summit, we'd need to abandon our plan for a fast one-day ascent. It would now take us at least two days. Rather than scurrying up with minimal gear, we would need to schlep heavier packs crammed with stoves, sleeping bags, and a tent, and spend a night squeezed onto an uncomfortable ledge halfway up the face. We'd also need to be more painstakingly methodical as we placed our boots on holds covered with ice and jammed our hands in cracks choked with snow. Sections that were easy when dry would require a lot more effort.

By the end of our conversation, Charley and I were reeling under all the new realities. The idea of totally changing our plan, our approach, and our expectations, was way too overwhelming. Maybe the face wouldn't be as difficult as we thought. Maybe we'd climb faster than anticipated. Maybe we'd get a perfect, bluebird day. Wasn't it supposed to be the dry season? In the end, despite all the game-changing facts thrown in our faces, I found myself packing for a one-day attempt.

So when the night sky actually appeared clear, we left at 3 AM and committed to an all-out push. We tried to feel positive and optimistic. I remember actually thinking that with a little luck, we might just make it. However, it's not often adversity throws you a bone.

About halfway up, the face began to change. As predicted, the cracks were choked with ice, and the lower angled faces were totally covered in snow, slowing us down to a crawl. It shouldn't have been a surprise when, about noontime, it started snowing and hailing.

We tried to hang tough, putting in an unbelievable effort to keep going. But two hours later, with melting snow running down the rock pouring icy water into our upturned sleeves, we were exhausted and getting cold fast. We knew we were beaten. Shivering, we made the long, demoralizing rappel down to camp and called off the climb. The good news is that the next year we came back and reached the summit under almost identical conditions.

Looking back, what defeated us on our first attempt was that we couldn't summon the resolve to take on the kind of climb that was required. The mountain wasn't going to change. The changes had to come from within us. However, the prospect of heavy packs weighing us down, the thought of a miserable night out on a ledge and starting the next morning with cold hands and feet, the contemplation of a ten-hour rappel through the cold and dark—all this was more than we could handle. If we had adjusted our course appropriately and been able to climb the entire face in those tough conditions, our sense of accomplishment would have been off the chart. Instead, not only did we go home empty-handed, but also we went home empty, knowing that we did not engage the mountain with the best parts of ourselves. Since then, I've learned a valuable lesson: It's not enough to face the facts. We need to act on them and to follow them where they lead us. By stepping into adversity, I've gained a whole new un-

You'd never know it, but my first attempt of Mount Kenya in 2005 was carefully planned for the dry season. Charley Mace and I were turned back by the rain, snow, and horrific conditions. However, we returned the next year with a third partner, Hans Florine, and under similar conditions reached the twin summits of Nelion and Batian after seventeen hours of nonstop climbing.

derstanding. From the moment I begin the ascent, I know that if I fully Take It On, I grow and deepen as a person, but it's seldom an easy climb.

The greatest people and teams *turn into the storm* when others step back. Rising to the occasion once or twice is admirable, but doing it over and over again, adjusting agilely with each and every adversity, requires more. It requires both immense will and sufficient skill, as well as developing new capabilities to rise up to the next challenge. And, ultimately, harnessing that adversity requires you to dig deep and summon your strengths, as you'll see in the next chapter.

Summon Your Strengths

ACONCAGUA

Base Camp: 14,000 feet
Summit: 22,841 feet
Aconcagua, located in Argentina, is the tallest peak in South America.

Whatever does not destroy me makes me stronger.

–FRIEDRICH NIETZSCHE

ROUTE DESCRIPTION

- ▶ Summit Strengths: Yours and Others'
- ▶ Human Will
- ▶ Your Greatest "Why"
- ▶ The Strength Formula
- ▶ Adversity Strengths versus Regular Strengths
  - • Closing the Gap
- ▶ The Team Advantage
- ▶ Synergy
- ▶ Choosing Your Team
  - • The AWE (Adversity, Why, and Ego) Factors
- ▶ Winning or Losing Depends on Your Goal

Erik

A lot of people buy into the idea that the best way to optimize your potential is to assess your natural strengths and then build your pursuits around them. Sure, natural strengths matter, but relying on them solely can be tragically limiting. Often the best things in life do not come naturally.

Beethoven went deaf later in life, and proceeded to write some of his greatest works. What if a life coach had encouraged him to pick a job "more befitting a deaf person"? Van Gogh was told he was an awful painter. What if he had listened to the critics? Einstein was labeled "academically ungifted" as a child. What if a school counselor had persuaded him to pursue a career involving manual labor instead of science? Countless business leaders, including Richard Branson of Virgin and John Chambers of Cisco, have dyslexia. What if they had accepted the "known limitations" of this diagnosis? And speaking personally, just how many blind climbers would there be? Consider all the masters who were once maladroit. Consider all the strengths lying within each of us, waiting to be summoned.

You should first decide what you want to do, why it's important, and whether you have the will to persevere. Then figure out what strengths you have or might be able to develop—from scratch, if necessary—to succeed. After that you need to try, struggle, fail, and fail again, until you get the results you're after. Let adversity be the flame in which your strengths are forged.

Focusing exclusively on what you're good at can actually be a subconscious way of avoiding the adversity that is implicit in every effort. Instead you want to use adversity to help you develop entirely new strengths and sharpen existing ones. Think of the times you faced a tough situation and emerged with a new confidence, a new insight, or perhaps even a deeper connection with the magnitude of your own resilience. My bet is you wouldn't trade those moments for anything. Neither would I.

Just as you can grow strengths through adversity, you've also got to be able to use them best when it hurts the most. An impressive array of

During my first Aconcagua ascent, the wind was so fierce and the terrain so rocky that we couldn't even hear each other's footsteps. I felt like I was not only blind, but deaf as well.

strengths means little unless you can deliver them in the face of real hardship. Do this, and they are truly yours.

Regardless of how many strengths you possess, it's almost impossible to achieve greatness alone. Linking with the right people can elevate the breadth and scope of your impact. Others will have strengths you do not, and skills that complement yours. However, the formula for picking your rope team is much more complex than simply inserting people into their proper spots based on their current abilities, like a snap-together puzzle.

Summit Two will help you with the tasks I had to do on Aconcagua: confront the brutal truth about what I currently was and was not good at, in the face of my highest aspirations, as well as determine what strengths my team and I needed to build in order to get where we wanted to go. This chapter will help you rethink your strengths so that you can bring forth your best in the toughest moments. You'll also learn how to build the strongest team to maximize your chance of success.

Aconcagua, the tallest peak in the Southern Hemisphere, highlighted all my weaknesses and few of my strengths. On McKinley, I could hear my climbing partners' footsteps crunching in the snow and ice in front of me, plus we were all roped together, so that following was easier. Aconcagua, though, is one of the windiest places on earth and mostly consists of rock and scree—the loose gravel that makes solid footing nearly impossible. When we were hiking across rock in the howling wind, the sound of footsteps was completely lost.

Also, McKinley was a smooth, steep plane of snow. Since I could predict my next steps, I was able to get into a good rhythm and save a lot of energy. But on Aconcagua I needed to constantly negotiate treacherous fields of boulders of all sizes, and devilish ice pinnacles called *penitentes,* which rise up five or six feet from the ground like twisted fangs. On other trails, I'd use long trekking poles to keep my balance and to feel my way; but on top of uneven boulders and penitentes, with huge deep zigzagging cracks between steps, I'd move at half the speed while putting forth double the effort. The consequences of a misstep would be a broken leg or worse.

The first time my team and I attempted Aconcagua, we failed to summit. We encountered extremely cold, blustery weather, which made it tougher to move our camps up the mountain. As a result, when the one clear, windless day finally came to Aconcagua, we weren't in position at our high camp and couldn't take advantage of it. The difficult terrain also had taken its toll on me. By the sixteenth day, when we finally went for the summit, I was exhausted and moving way too slowly. At 21,000 feet, with fierce winds blasting us, I couldn't hear my climbing partner Chris Morris in front of me anymore. I felt disoriented and a little panicky—not just blind, but now deaf as well. Chris gathered us together to shout that the climb was over. The mountain and the weather were just too much for our collective abilities. It was such a difficult and miserable trip that most of my friends weren't even interested in trying again. Also, being slowed down by a blind partner probably didn't provide much incentive for another attempt. But Chris was game.

I was determined to use this adversity—our failure—to our advantage, but I knew that by itself my will would not be enough. I needed to evolve new techniques for negotiating this hostile terrain. During the next year, I set about developing the skills that I lacked—those I knew I needed if we were ever going to succeed on Aconcagua. I practiced on the slopes of Colorado's "fourteeners"—14,000-foot peaks—which have a rocky terrain similar to Aconcagua. Chris and I developed a new mode of communication with a bear bell, which Chris would jingle to the left or right, helping me to follow through wind and over rock. I honed my pole work to balance more effectively in precarious spots. Also, I created a new technique: I'd stand on a boulder and, with my back leg in a deep knee bend, would probe out with the other foot to find the next boulder. Then I'd reach my poles across the large gap, plant them where I wanted to step, and pole-vault my way across. I trained hard with extra weight in my pack so I could really travel fast if we had to.

Chris and I practiced over and over and over, knowing it wouldn't be enough to master these new skills in calm conditions. We had to make them work in the worst weather. And we got our chance. The ferocious

Colorado winds repeatedly blasted away at us, and I worked at calming my mind in the midst of their fury as we pushed toward different summits on exposed ridges. I was still working harder than the others and having to concentrate more, but no one ever guaranteed me that life was going to be fair or easy, and I didn't really care. I was just grateful that I could find a way to be doing the thing I loved.

Then we regrouped and took on Aconcagua a second time. Right out of Base Camp, Chris and I lost our only other teammate, who descended because of acute altitude sickness. It was just the two of us, and as Chris so clearly stated, "Now we cannot afford to make *any* mistakes."

Just as in the previous year, the weather was marginal, but we kept pushing our camps up the mountain, knowing that this time we had to be in position for the summit when the weather turned fair. One day we felt so strong, we skipped an intermediate camp and climbed almost 4,000 feet to the next camp.

On summit day at 21,000 feet, we encountered even worse winds than the year before: sixty miles per hour. The previous year, I had started the morning overdressed and gotten wet with sweat. When I hit the wind, the dampness had instantly evaporated, taking my body heat with it, and I was suddenly cold. This time I dressed lightly and had all my extra clothes organized and ready. When the time came, we huddled behind a rock and put on everything we had to fend off the wind, with only limited success.

As we struggled up the ridge, Chris's bell, which had been work-ing great until then, must have frozen, because I could no longer hear it—just when I needed it most. We were being blown back and contem-plated retreating. But we had trained enough and had become skilled enough to keep pushing on, with the idea that if we could battle through the wind, we'd enter a calmer zone around the leeward side of the moun-tain.

Chris knew I couldn't hear his yells, so for three hours he'd turn around, banging his pole against rocks and putting his bare fingers in his mouth to whistle loudly. For me, all that training with extra weight was paying off. At 21,500 feet, the wind abated, but the cold intensified. When I stumbled onto the rocky summit, the extreme altitude, along with my complete exhaustion, made my connection with the earth feel tenuous, as if I were perceiving reality through a distant pinhole. But we were on top, finally, after two years of trying.

When I eventually got back to "high camp," I collapsed in the frozen dirt, lying there with half of me convinced that I wasn't cut out for this life. I wasn't tough enough. I wasn't resilient enough. And besides, what a ridiculous pursuit for a guy who couldn't see! But the other half of me couldn't imagine doing anything else with my life. I wanted to climb forever.

I once had a college professor who claimed that human beings are the only species in the entire animal kingdom who dream beyond their limitations. I find this an admirable quality. To settle into our obvious strengths and the paths where they lead us is to slash from our psyches our deepest yearnings, our highest aspirations, and those transformative qualities that define alchemy.

A year earlier, in better weather, we couldn't make it to the summit, but we used that failure to grow stronger and more adept. The tougher it got, the better we got. Together, our will and our skill forged new strengths that got us to a place most people thought we'd never reach. Through adversity, we equipped ourselves for bigger challenges to come. You can, too.

Paul

Summit Strengths: Yours and Others'

I don't measure a man's success by how high he climbs,
but by how high he bounces when he hits bottom.
—GEORGE PATTON

What role have you let adversity play in your life? Are you willing to struggle, fail, and fail again? Do you, like Erik, use adversity to

After our disappointing failure on Aconcagua, I trained for a year in stormy weather on 14,000-foot peaks in the Rockies, learning the skills I had lacked on my first try. The next year, Chris Morris and I finally reached the 22,841-foot summit in extreme cold and high winds.

forge new strengths, or do you rely on those you naturally have? How effectively do you develop new strengths?

Equally important, *when* do you summon your strengths? Which strengths come through when the weather is calm, as opposed to when the weather is rough? When do you feel the strongest? When the pressure is on, how does your behavior affect the degree to which others trust and respect you? When adversity strikes, what can people count on you to deliver?

In order to get the best results you cannot possibly go it alone, so what about your *team*? Do your team members both summon and develop their strengths through adversity? Do they all bring out their best when it matters most? Or do people slip into default mode, resorting to protective, safer, less effective behavior when the pressure is on?

Every business I work with, regardless of industry, struggles to summon the strengths of its employees in order to move toward its vision. The ability—or lack of ability—to do so determines success over the long haul. What difficulties have you and your team surmounted? Do the members of your team have strengths that complement each other? How effectively do you weave together your individual strengths to create collective greatness? What challenge have you and your team hesitated to take on, maybe because you're not convinced that you collectively possess the strengths it would take to succeed? What if you could take on this challenge—and succeed?

Summit Two is about developing the strengths you have, as well as new ones, so you can bring them forth in times of adversity to accomplish what you set out to do. People who successfully use adversity as fuel don't just rely on their existing strengths. They constantly and relentlessly develop areas that others once labeled as their weaknesses. They recognize that expanding their capabilities gives them greater traction, momentum, and options.

But having the right strengths is not, by itself, sufficient. You turn adversity to your advantage by bringing out your best in the toughest situations. As Erik says, "You don't have to be the best. You just have to be darn good when it really counts."

Human Will

> *Strength does not come from physical capacity.*
> *It comes from an indomitable will.*
>
> —MAHATMA GANDHI

Willpower is synonymous with self-control. You exercise your willpower when you stop smoking. *Will* is determination in action. Of Erik's many qualities, it is his sheer human will to do the thing he sets out to do that most people find incredibly inspiring. Seeing it in action, whether on a television special or in one of his award-winning films, or better yet in person, is truly humbling. A common response to meeting Erik and hearing his story is "It pretty much kills any excuses I have for not . . ."

When your will is stoked, it overwhelms excuses with conviction, effort, and action. Will can drive everyday greatness, because it spurs you to do the right but difficult thing that others might back down from doing. And it takes significant will to accomplish your Summit Challenge.

At any level, *will* includes *determination, desire, decisiveness,* and *effort.* Altogether, will is a formidable force that can overcome, even overpower, other winning traits such as intelligence, charisma, and curiosity. To be strong-willed about something is to put your force of conviction and relentless effort behind it—to want it, focus on it, decide it must be done, and then do it.

Yet people hedge their bets every day. They believe that to show conviction is to risk disappointment or ridicule if they fail. I believe that to withhold conviction is to sacrifice everyday greatness. Will has enormous power. That's why it is so vital to channel your will toward something that ultimately elevates you and others.

Your Greatest "Why"

He who has a strong enough why *can bear almost any* how.
—FRIEDRICH NIETZSCHE

In Summit One, you picked the most compelling thing that you always wanted to do, the single accomplishment that would excite, enrich, inspire, and improve you; one that will build capacity, benefit others, and fuel greatness. Your Summit Challenge connects to your greatest "why." We all want our brief time here to matter, to be significant. Your "why" has a huge influence on your will. The more compelling your "why," the more adversity you will weather for the cause. Your highest, most compelling reason for your Summit Challenge will help guide you through the cold, dark night of adversity.

We've all seen people with tremendous ability fail in an environment or in a pursuit for which they have no compelling motivation. Many teenagers, even though they are bright and academic, don't succeed in college because they don't see the point of doing the work required. Others will recognize that college is not an end, but a beginning. They will do what they have to in order to have more options available to them, to graduate and move on to bigger and better opportunities. When we have a compelling "why," it's amazing how we can summon the will to do what needs to be done.

Opposite the underachievers are those inspiring people who, like Erik, prevail under circumstances in which failure could easily be understood. For example, Kellie Lim has a strong desire to help sick children. Kellie knows firsthand what it is like to be hospitalized as a child. Due to bacterial meningitis, she was a triple amputee by the age of eight, losing both legs below the knees and one arm below the elbow. One medical school told her not to even bother applying, which only fueled her determination! Her will also was intensified by the example of her mother, Sandy, who had gone blind in her twenties. Other than being unable to drive, Sandy made life as normal as possible for her three children. She cooked, kept house, and walked the kids to school. Kellie Lim, saying that she simply wanted to repay the kindness she had received when she was a sick child, graduated from UCLA medical school in 2007.

The Strength Formula

In Summit One, you pinpointed your most important Summit Challenge, the single adversity that, once conquered, would produce the greatest and deepest positive changes in your life. Now it's time to ask yourself what strengths you need to make it happen. Which strengths do you already possess, and which do you need to develop?

A skill that is practiced becomes a strength. My formula: *will* plus *skill* equals *strength*.

- ▶ Will is important but, by itself, is not enough to achieve everyday greatness. You also need a certain degree of skill. If you desire to be a race car driver, but you are extremely nearsighted and have poor reflexes, your will alone is unlikely to make your dream come true.
- ▶ At the same time, an innate skill, talent, or natural gift can be extremely helpful, but only when you have the will to use it. Let's

imagine a set of twins, both of whom are facile with numbers. After college they are immediately hired by an insurance company for their math skills. One loves actuarial tables, spends long hours analyzing data, makes a brilliant discovery about the mathematical relationship between life expectancy and shoe size, and goes on to become an insurance magnate. The other really prefers raising orchids and moves to Hawaii.

Many people assume that fabulous musicians are natural-born prodigies, and the rest of us can never acquire their level of skill. In fact, studies have shown that the most successful musicians are not necessarily those who were born with the most talent, but those who are willing to put in the longest hours practicing. That is, they have a certain amount of talent, plus tremendous will that keeps them practicing and practicing after other musicians sign off.

When you work relentlessly to improve your skill, it becomes a genuine strength upon which you can rely when times get tough.

Adversity Strengths versus Regular Strengths

Now you are ready to explore who you are and what you bring out not when times are calm, but when the world is turbulent and adversity rules the day. Most people possess two kinds of strengths:

1. *Regular Strengths* are those qualities you regularly demonstrate under calm, normal conditions.
2. *Adversity Strengths* are those that rise up and shine when you're under the gun or feeling the pressure, or when the situation goes south. These are the strengths that help you effectively take on each new challenge.

If you are like most people, many of your strengths are apparent under ideal conditions, such as a celebration, vacation, or when life is clicking along. You may be a riot at parties, a joy on holidays, or an incredible leader as the company flourishes. These may be the times when you are the best at listening, being creative, making people laugh, connecting with others, being spontaneous, solving problems, getting things done, or just being a positive influence on others. But how apparent are these strengths when you're under significant or extended pressure and strain?

Closing the Gap

Some people have nearly identical Regular and Adversity Strengths. Other people do not. The strengths they bring forth in calmer times are completely different from those they demonstrate when the wind is howling or the heat is on. Examining the difference can be a wake-up call.

If you are two distinctly separate people depending on the circumstances, then there is no real connection between "the calm you" and "the stressed you," and your strengths are situational. If there is complete overlap between your Regular Strengths and Adversity Strengths, then you demonstrate exceptional dependability. For example, if you are compassionate in both calm times and tough times, then people trust you to be compassionate no matter what.

It is quite common for people to change when adversity strikes. Their Regular Strengths step back, and—assuming they actually possess some—their Adversity Strengths step up. If the contrast is extreme enough, people can feel as if they are dealing with someone who is almost bipolar. Others remain on guard, wondering *which* self is going to emerge, and *when*.

Closing the gap between your Regular and Adversity Strengths pays huge dividends in all relationships and will heighten the trust and respect others have for you. I encourage you to begin closing the gap by making two separate lists:

1. List all of those attributes the people who know you best would say you demonstrate under calm or "normal" circumstances.
2. List those attributes the people who know you best would say you demonstrate most consistently and effectively when you are under pressure or faced with adversity. How would they complete the sentence "Whenever something bad happens, you always . . . ?"

If you're having trouble thinking of specific strengths to write down, what follows is an abbreviated list derived from Christopher Peterson and Martin Seligman's book *Character Strengths and Virtues*. You also may think of additional attributes, or strengths that defy categorization.

- ▶ Relationships—Strengths related to your ability to understand, connect with, form, and maintain relationships with other people.
- ▶ Creativity (ingenuity, originality)—Strengths in arts, invention, ideas, innovations, design, and more.
- ▶ Attitude/Outlook—Strengths related to outlook, energy, optimism, perspective, open-mindedness.
- ▶ Virtues—Strengths related to honesty, fairness, restraint, selflessness, courage, and more.
- ▶ Thinking—Cognitive abilities related to how you think about things.
- ▶ Physical—Strengths related to coordination, fine motor skills, stamina, flexibility, movement, and more.
- ▶ Spiritual—Strengths related to sensing, connecting with, tapping into the higher level of the world around you.

When my wife, Ronda, says to me, "Whenever something bad happens, you get incredibly focused," she's highlighting an Adversity Strength. It's something that is particularly noticeable to her when I'm under stress.

Once you've got your two lists, you are ready to compare them, examine the discrepancies, and begin to consider how you will close the gaps so you are reliable under pressure. Look for the gaps that cause you or others the most difficulty. It's easy to identify the most obvious ones. If you're nice when things are going well, and surly when things are going badly, the contrast is unmistakable.

What strengths do you currently *lack* in the face of adversity—strengths that, if you demonstrated them, would fuel your everyday greatness? For example, I am capable of showing patience when everything is serene. But under pressure, such as an urgent deadline, a missed flight, or a fleeting opportunity, I move fast and have little patience for people or things that move slowly. I'm not proud of this, but it has been my default mode my whole life. Formerly when people mentioned it, I rationalized their observations away, thinking privately, "I'm not being impatient. I'm just being appropriately intense and effective." But by the time the third person used the phrase "really impatient," I knew I had a gap that needed to be addressed. If I could demonstrate greater patience when under pressure, it would help me be more magnanimous and connected with the people around me when magnanimity and connection really matter.

How do we close the gap and create new Adversity Strengths? It's simple, but not easy. It's enriching, and humbling, because you'll bump up against your very nature and realize how your behavior ripples out across situations in ways you never intended.

Closing the gap requires you to be brutally honest with yourself. Personally, I engage the people around me who are most likely to be present at, if not directly involved with, the next adversity. It's not always best to ask your subordinates, since you may unintentionally be putting them in a terrible predicament. I simply approach people directly with my request: "Listen, I recognize I'm not as patient as I would like to be with you and everyone else when we're under the gun. I am really committed to doing better, and I would like to ask for your help. Next time I'm impatient with you or anyone else in a bad way, I'd really appreciate if you'd alert me that I need to slow down and do better. And please know, while I may not appear pleased when you do it, and I may slip up, I *am* grateful, and I *will* listen."

The important thing, of course, is to honor your commitments to those who are helping you—and never, ever shoot the messenger! It's also a nice gesture to thank people for their role. Being able to pinpoint, address, and take action in an area in which you seek to improve is a sign of everyday greatness. Chances are you'll inspire others to do the same. That's good leadership. Closing the gap between your Regular Strengths and your Adversity Strengths is a powerful way to help you bring out more of your best in *all* situations.

The Team Advantage

As we apply these principles and tools, it's important for you to know that Erik's teams have been some of the best in the world. On Mount Everest, for instance, not only did Erik become the only blind climber to reach the summit, but his team made history, too. Typically, 10 percent of climbers reach the summit. Erik's team applied their Adversity Strengths to bring nineteen out of twenty-one team members to the top. That's the most people from one team to reach the top of Everest in a single day. *Time* magazine called Erik's team one of the greatest ever to climb the mountain. The accomplishment serves as a perfect allegory for what is possible for your team. So how did they do it?

Erik's team had no superstar, no world-renowned climbers. The team had normal people—including an architect, two doctors, a physician's assistant, a teacher, and a geophysicist—who accomplished something together that far transcended anything any of them had ever done before.

In contrast, think about all the teams you've encountered that had enormous talent but fell short. The classic case is the United States 2004 men's Olympic basketball "Dream Team," composed of top-paid, marquee-name professionals and the hottest college recruits in the nation. The team entered the games in Greece as the landslide favorite. Each player was a clear standout in his position, boasting incredible personal stats and numerous team championships. How could the Dream Team possibly lose? It had the top talent, and the United States had won the gold in twelve of the past fourteen Olympics. For many Americans, this Dream Team was synonymous with gold. Imagine the crushing blow they experienced when the team lost by nineteen points to Puerto Rico in the opening round, went on to lose two more games, and had to settle for a bronze medal, standing below two far less talented teams.

Assembling talented people cannot guarantee success. When Erik decided to take on Everest, he had to look for special qualities in the people he selected. He needed team members with an enormous ability to deliver their best while under adversity. He looked for people with a clear, compelling reason *why* they were eager to suffer through such an epic feat. It had to be about more than just conquering a mountain. And he needed people with enough self-confidence to take on a challenge some might call impossible, but not so much confidence that it exceeded their actual strengths.

Erik

Synergy

Individual strengths only go so far, and it's impossible to possess, or to grow, every strength you need to tackle every important challenge single-handedly. Few of your grandest aspirations can be achieved alone.

No matter how good I became at climbing, I never could have made it to the top of the Seven Summits without my team. With each new expedition, I turn to others for the complementary strengths required for the challenge. In fact, one of the unexpected benefits of going blind was that it forced me to confront my limitations and to begin surrounding myself with people who could help me grow and make me a better person. In my early years, I desperately strove to be independent, but when I began climbing mountains, I experienced an evolution far more beautiful and powerful than independence. It was inter*dependence.*

The only way to cross a glacier on a mountain is to form a rope team. The complete and utter commitment involved in making that rope team function is one of the most inspiring facets of any climb. If it's a good rope team, you wriggle up the mountain like a snake, all the parts in perfect sync, yet each person performing a distinct and vital function. If one person falls through a snow bridge or takes a tumble, it's in everyone's best interest to quickly stop that person from going any farther. You throw yourself down onto your ice axe and arrest his plummet, as he would yours. This is not something you stop to think about. It's automatic.

That commitment to each other is based on enormous trust. In some ways it's terrifying, because there's no middle ground. You win together or you lose together. You know you can drive the team forward or kill it. Everyone's fate becomes inextricably linked to everyone else's. When there are high points, you share them, and when there are difficulties, which there always are, you face them head-on together.

When you're roped up, someone's always going to have a bad day.

When you're feeling low and moving slowly, inevitably you'll feel the rope in front of you grow taut. In rope team lingo, that's called, "Haulin' tuna." One day you're hauling tuna, and the next day you're the tuna getting hauled. Knowing you affect the ones you care about makes you hang in there and climb better.

My climbing partner, Jeff Evans, is from the South. His granddaddy once gave Jeff his expert wisdom on rope teams. "Now I know why you all rope up," he said. "It's to keep the smart ones from turning tail and going home!"

There are no shortcuts to becoming an effective and interdependent team. The benefits are hard-earned, but in an environment riddled with pitfalls, roping up with good people can be a powerful tool. At the team level, you go through the same steps as an individual. You begin with an exciting and worthwhile Summit Challenge. The team members frankly talk through all the obstacles. Then you sort, assemble, and develop the strengths you'll need to rise to the challenge. As you prepare together and suffer together, even fail together, you slowly build upon each other's strengths until the team begins to take on an organic quality, the whole more powerful than its parts.

Paul

Choosing Your Team

How do you select a team like this that will win in the face of adversity? Go for AWE.

The A Factor: Adversity Strengths

The A Factor has to do with how people perform and what strengths they bring forth while facing adversity. It is a gauge of how effective, consistent, and dependable a person is when the pressure's on. You can probably imagine immediately how important the A Factor is in the people in your personal life. But what about its effect at work?

In business, I see companies struggle terribly with the question of hiring—whom they should "get on the bus," as the noted business author Jim Collins says. At the very least you're probably looking for someone who is honest and dependable, with a good work ethic and the desire to succeed. But do you choose a track record with proven skills over untested talent and potential? Is IQ more important than personality and emotional intelligence? You will undoubtedly evaluate every aspect of job candidates you can, from their appearance and social skills to their values and cultural beliefs. But will you remember to gauge their Adversity Strengths?

Erik takes prospective new team members out on trail climbs and mini-adventures, where the climbers are subtly checked out to see how well they handle the tough stuff, as an indication of their A Factor on a more serious climb. You, too, can put people into challenging situations, or take note when such situations happen to arise, and gauge the way they behave under pressure. The more realistic the trial, the better the evaluation.

If you're serious about hiring certain candidates, ask them how they see their own Adversity Strengths. Then ask others for examples that illustrate how these candidates handled adversity in the past. Do the two viewpoints match? Now you have a better idea about not only the candidates' strengths, but also how well they know themselves. Try to determine both which Adversity Strengths the candidates demonstrate under pressure and chronic stress, and also which Adversity Strengths they need to develop.

As we read Erik's amazing tales of harnessing adversity, we need to remember that we all suffer from our own form of blindness. It's difficult for us to see with perfect clarity our own strengths and shortcomings. Some people overestimate what they have to offer, while others underestimate their contribution. Either way, there are usually discrepancies between the way we see ourselves and the way others see us. You put yourself and your team in a much stronger position when you gain utter clarity about your Adversity Strengths, and you help others to shed light on theirs. If, as a result of this book, you become more deliberate in assessing the A Factor of the people you invite to join your "rope team," then your time will have been richly invested.

The W Factor: Why?

It's so informative to ask a candidate, "*Why* do you want to be a part of this team?" Then come back again with "Yes, I understand, but *why*?" I find that by the fourth or fifth "why," you get at the real reason, the answer that rings true, the "why" beneath the "why." The intensity of this response is that person's W Factor. Consider it to be a major warning sign if this "why" is anemic, self-centered, or small. But if it is authentic, uplifting, heartfelt, and compelling, chances are it will engage the deepest pools of this person's will.

The E Factor: Ego

The word *ego* has various connotations, but for this discussion it refers to someone's idea of his or her own importance or worth. The question is, what is the relationship between a person's self-confidence and his or her actual strengths? Sure, we're all put off by people whose egos far exceed their capabilities, to the point they can't fit through the doorway, or simply suck all the air out of a room. But there are two kinds of ego: *unsubstantiated* ego, and *substantiated* ego.

Imagine you have a teenage daughter, and her new boyfriend, Rip, just came to the door to pick her up. He is skinny, with dark hair that he appears to have cut himself with blunt scissors. He has his hands stuck in his pockets and is wearing an old coat and black sneakers. He has a tattoo on his neck that you can't quite make out, and possibly some eyeliner. Your daughter says brightly that Rip is in a band and he is going to go far, just as soon as he gets out of his parents' house. Rip says he has almost signed a contract with a record label, his latest CD is wicked awesome, and his band is really pumped about it. You're thinking Rip is a cocky little you-know-what. While your daughter is out, you listen to Rip's CD and discover that:

1. It is the most brain-numbingly terrible garage rock you have ever heard. Too bad—Rip has an *unsubstantiated* ego. Or,

2. The band is incredibly talented and clearly has put tremendous effort into their first album. Congratulations—Rip has a *substantiated* ego.

Don't automatically be put off by someone with a healthy (substantiated) ego. It just might prove vital to your cause. Erik points out that most of the great climbers he invites onto his rope team have big egos. They're amazing climbers, and they know it. Imagine if they were overly humble and failed to realize how capable they really are. As soon as the next unexpected challenge arose, they might back down, rather than rise up, when it matters most.

Those who perceive themselves as less capable are likely to lower their sights to more pedestrian goals. It takes a certain degree of ego, or chutzpah, or moxie, to even consider going after lofty goals. To take full advantage of adversity, you need inner strength. Ego can be what fortifies you with the self-confidence you need to take risks, to take on the daunting or impossible, and to step up when others step back. Personally, I would not want anyone on my team without a healthy, substantiated ego. They need it!

Erik

Winning or Losing Depends on Your Goal

After picking the members of my Everest team, the next step was to test ourselves in a real Himalayan environment. So my team of thirteen attempted Ama Dablam, a steep, formidable peak located in the Khumbu region of Nepal, just a few miles from its taller, more famous cousin. When I look back, I realize that if my team had not faced this ascent together a year earlier, chances are we never would have reached the summit of Everest. Adversity was the teacher that elevated us from a bunch of skilled friends with the desire to climb together to a true team capable of doing something great when it really mattered.

This talented group of individuals, assembled together for the first time, immediately climbed pretty well as a team, with people gravitating toward their natural strengths, as they so often do. We had technical experts, or "rope guns," using their functional brilliance to get out in front, fixing lines up the ridgeline and sheer faces. We had analytical experts using their knack for detail to plan all the moving parts of the ascent. And we had the "grunts" like me, using their endurance and strength to slog heavy gear. After three weeks in favorable conditions, we had made great time, setting up a camp at 21,000 feet. In retrospect, I see that we were only using our calm weather strengths, but circumstances were about to change.

The next day the monsoons began to roar in unexpectedly early in the season. They layered the mountain with snow and ice, giving us only a couple hours of sunlight to climb each morning before the daily onslaught. Because we all had mountain experience, none of us was fazed. If you want to climb big mountains, facing some harsh weather is part of the deal.

Because climbing up and down the steep rocky face was starting to beat me up, we made some adjustments. Eric Alexander and I chose to stay at the 21,000-foot camp while the rest of the team went back down to Base Camp to wait out the storms. Eric and I were ultimately stuck up

Ama Dablam is a steep, formidable cousin of Mount Everest. My team and I hoped that taking it on would build the team strengths that might carry us to the top of the world.

there for eight days with ice and rocks crashing down around our tent. The campsite was so small, the tent's right corner hung precariously over a 3,000-foot cliff. I let Eric sleep on that side.

Finally, the rest of the team fought their way back up to us. We immediately drew upon the expertise of our rope guns to set climbing lines up higher so we could continue our ascent, but the long wait had cut too far into our resources. We were running out of the food and fuel we had set aside for our summit push. Facing no respite in the horrible conditions, Pasquale (PV) Scaturro, our team leader, made the difficult call to turn us back. Although we had bonded, and we had demonstrated that each of us possessed the ability and fortitude to climb, our effort so far had done little to convince me one way or the other that this group had what it would take to succeed on Mount Everest.

As the team carefully rappelled downward, everything was now covered in ice, even our ropes. We named one particularly scary section Abject Terror, after a famous quote from climbing literature: "Mountaineering is extended periods of intense boredom, interrupted by occasional moments of abject terror." It was a slick, thirty-foot traverse across vertical rock on a fixed line, our fifty-pound packs pulling us backward over thousands of feet of space with hardly any handholds or footholds. On top of that, another afternoon storm swept in. Now the wind was picking us up and slamming us back against the rocks.

Far below me, Eric, judging himself to be in a safe spot, detached himself from the line and stepped on a rock that immediately dislodged and sent him careening 150 feet down a rock face. He was banged up badly, but everyone breathed a sigh of relief when he waved to signal that he was okay. However, the fall had dramatically shocked his system and soon his lungs began gurgling with each breath, a sign of a severe form of altitude illness that can quickly kill.

Getting Eric down the mountain in his impaired state would be hazardous, demanding the teams' very best Adversity Strengths. Calm weather strengths now meant nothing. Steve Gipe, our unhurried, slow-talking team doctor, always the last into camp, showed the most dramatic transformation. He sped up tenfold as he rapidly rappelled down the mountain face and scrambled across the boulder fields below to retrieve the oxygen bottles we had stashed for emergencies. Suddenly this teammate we all thought of as dreamy and laid-back became clear-eyed and laser-focused. In no time he had an oxygen mask over Eric's face and kept him moving, despite the fact that Eric was sitting down every twenty feet, near collapse.

The rest of the team kicked into high gear, too, as we relayed heavy loads across treacherous sections of the ridge. Later, team members took turns talking me down the ice-coated face. Different friends stepped in to relieve each other without any prompting. I was bleary with exhaustion and lack of sleep, but as we struggled downward in the wind and cold, it was as though we had stepped out of our individual roles and had morphed into one cohesive unit. The team had taken on a life force of its own.

It was about midnight when we straggled into Base Camp together, utterly spent. The adrenaline had long worn off, and all we wanted was to pile into our sleeping bags, but there was much more work to do.

Steve had already zipped Eric inside our Gamow (pronounced "gam-off") bag, a portable hyperbaric oxygen chamber equipped with a foot pump, in hopes of helping Eric stabilize. But the pressure inside the chamber had to remain constant. So, despite our exhaustion, we took shifts sitting by the bag, regularly pumping air into it throughout the night and into the next day. Luckily there was a brief patch of clear weather, and we called in a helicopter that carried Eric down to safety.

Back in Kathmandu, we met with the statistician who keeps a record of Himalayan expeditions. After jotting some notes, she turned to me and asked, "If you couldn't summit Ama Dablam, what makes you think you have a chance on Everest?" The question implied that we had tried something pretty bold and had utterly and completely failed. But I felt differently.

If we had summited in perfect weather, we wouldn't have learned as much about what we could achieve as a team. Instead we had faced the perfect combination of adversity—terrible conditions, real danger, lack of resources, and complete exhaustion—to bring out our collective Adversity Strengths. The mountain had erected powerful barricades in our path, and

Teammate Eric Alexander, badly banged up from his fall on Ama Dablam, went into shock and needed to be placed in a Gamow bag, a portable hyperbaric oxygen chamber that must be constantly kept inflated by a foot pump. Inside, it simulates a lower altitude, which helps alleviate the symptoms of severe altitude sickness. We had to pump air into the bag for two days until a break in the storm allowed a helicopter to land at Base Camp and fly Eric to safety.

one by one we had torn them down, becoming a real team. Through these adversities, we had forged the strengths that we knew might just carry us to the top of the world.

I thought not only about the formidable physical challenges that lay ahead, but also about the inner strength I would need to take on Everest. From my previous climbing experiences, I had developed a certain level of mental toughness, and I had learned a great deal about my Adversity Strengths. I knew intuitively that Everest would call for critical mental skills that, I discovered later, Paul referred to as CORE abilities. By engaging the CORE skills described in the next chapter—the ability to focus on the things we can influence, the willingness to take action to make the best of tough situations, the resolve to minimize any potential downside as well as to maximize any upside, and the endurance to work relentlessly to get through the suffering—I have been able to shatter my own perceptions of what is possible.

Engage Your CORE

MOUNT EVEREST

Base Camp: 17,500 feet
Summit: 29,028 feet
Mount Everest, located in Nepal and Tibet,
is the tallest peak in Asia—and the world.

There's nothing either good or bad, but thinking makes it so.
—WILLIAM SHAKESPEARE

ROUTE DESCRIPTION

- ► Understanding Your Adversity Quotient (AQ)
- ► Your CORE
  - • Control . . . Ownership . . . Reach . . . Endurance
- ► Raising Your Adversity Quotient
  - • Celebrating Stepping-Stones . . . The Summit Game . . . The Failure Fantasy . . . Positive Pessimism
- ► Building Your CORE
  - • Ask for Feedback . . . Your CORE Awareness . . . Recognize CORE Elements in Action . . . Employ the CORE Strategy . . . Create a CORE Action Plan
- ► Ernest Shackleton

Erik

You've already learned about facing adversity head-on, and the importance of being able to summon your strengths when you need them the most. But what if your "climb" is riddled with paralyzing levels of uncertainty? What do you do when some of the most important factors are completely out of your control, when the adversity is too great, when the level of hardship you have to endure renders the goal no longer worth pursuing, or when the goal you set out to achieve appears genuinely impossible? The reality is that anyone trying to achieve everyday greatness faces these moments of doubt almost daily. Most people back down or break. But there are a rare few who prevail and emerge stronger and better as a result. I've always been intrigued by the difference.

What I've discovered through Paul's research is that there is an inner mechanism or switch, deep within you, that can be triggered whenever adversity strikes. You can rewire your response to adversity by using a new set of tools that allow you to take advantage of the hardships that invariably come with attempting anything big and worthwhile. This switch has sparked powers in me that I never knew I possessed, and it can do the same for you.

I was truly tested when I faced the greatest challenge of my climbing career, right above Base Camp on Mount Everest. The Khumbu Icefall is a blind person's worst nightmare—2,000 vertical feet of jumbled ice boulders, ranging in size from baseballs to skyscrapers, all chaotically piled up. The Icefall is created by the glacier that pushes down the mountain ever so slowly and, upon reaching a giant cliff, collapses under its own weight, tumbling and exploding like a river of ice.

Even before entering the Icefall, I could hear the looming, fragile ice towers shifting and cracking over my head like an army of grim reapers. The forces at play in the Icefall were enormous, and completely out of my control. It was chaos: with no two steps ever being the same, I had to climb up ice walls and down the other side, weaving along a trail a foot wide next to

By 8 AM, we reached the South Summit of Mount Everest at 28,700 feet, only 200 feet below the true summit, but still two hours away and the most difficult climbing ahead. Above this point I played the Summit Game, envisioning myself and my team on top.

a 1,000-foot drop jumping from ice boulder to ice boulder as they rocked under my feet.

To make matters worse, there were dozens of cracks or crevasses zigzagging through the Icefall, and we had to either jump over them or walk a tightrope over narrow snow bridges. Sometimes the crevasses were so wide I couldn't feel the other side with my trekking poles. The only way across was a literal leap of faith. The members of my climbing team would tap their own poles on the opposite bank where they wanted me to land. Then I'd jump, knowing if I was off even a few inches, I'd shatter a kneecap or break an ankle.

To enhance the torture, there were dozens of crevasses so wide you couldn't cross them by jumping. For these, the Sherpas would lay aluminum construction ladders across the gap that the rest of the team needed to cross safely and efficiently. Sometimes there were five ladders lashed together with thin nylon rope, or what I liked to call "Sherpa Kmart boat twine." I had practiced back home on ladders propped up on cinder blocks a foot off the ground, but when I stood on the real thing, with the ladders being buffeted by the wind and the middle sagging over a hundred foot chasm, it was a whole different world.

My first trip through the Icefall took me thirteen hours. It was the hardest day of my life in the mountains. When I finally struggled above it and neared Camp One at 20,000 feet, I wasn't sure which was more trashed, my mind or my body. For those excruciating thirteen hours, I knew I could not make a mistake, yet I was never 100 percent sure that with my next step I wouldn't drop off into space. Then, as I was nearing camp, I broke through the snow and sank into a tiny crevasse. A teammate reached out to grab me but accidentally blasted me in the nose with the handle of his ice axe. So as I staggered into camp, not only was I green with nausea and about to pass out, but I had globs of blood dripping down my face.

Finally in my tent, I couldn't imagine crossing the Icefall once more, let alone the ten additional times that would be required to acclimatize to the altitude and to shuttle loads to the higher camps. I heard PV gathering the team outside to quietly tell them I was moving way too slowly. "If he takes

People assume it's not as scary climbing blind because I can't see the drop-offs. In truth, the prospect of falling into the unknown is even more terrifying. My first steps across this swaying ladder pushed my fear-meter higher than it's ever gone. But there's no way to reach the top of Everest without taking on adversity.

thirteen hours instead of six, he has twice the chance of getting hit by fall-ing ice, and so does anyone who is with him. Worse, the odds increase in the afternoon heat. If he can't find a way to get through significantly faster, he'll have to go down."

As I fell asleep that night, I began hearing these internal voices I came to know as the "Sirens." They called out to me and taunted me, saying, "If you can barely make it through the Icefall, you don't have a chance up higher. You gave it your best shot, but you're way outmatched. Go down while you still can. Besides, there are cheeseburgers and warm beds wait-ing for you."

In the *Odyssey,* the warrior Odysseus is sailing home from the Trojan War when he passes the Island of the Sirens—beautiful maidens who call out to Odysseus and his sailors with such alluring, melodious voices that the men become completely spellbound. They dive off the ship and swim furiously to the island, where they realize, to their horror, that the maidens are really monsters. They are never seen or heard from again. Odysseus, knowing the power of the Sirens, stuffs wax in his ears and has himself tied to the mast of the ship. Even then, their call is so seductive, he almost goes insane.

The adversity I faced on Everest seemed so enormous, terrible, and unending that my brain simply pushed the panic button. I knew I had to rise to the challenge. I told myself over and over that the Sirens were my brain's defense mechanism gone haywire. They were monsters, lurking at the base of the mountain, waiting to gobble up my desire, my ambition, my very will.

Whenever we face a great challenge, especially one racked with un-certainty, we contemplate the months of hard work, struggle, sacrifice, risk, and all the dangers lurking around each corner, and it's easy to become overwhelmed. What saved me was a beautiful Tibetan saying I had heard during our ceremony at Base Camp: "The nature of mind is like water. If you do not disturb it, it will become clear." I thought a lot about that.

I had been preparing for this climb half my life. I had trained for two years and had surrounded myself with the best people possible. I knew what to do, but what was about to turn me back was my own mind, cloudy with fear and doubt. To give myself a chance, I had to clear my mind, to "still" it like water. Everest, like all mountains, had to be climbed step-by-step, moment by moment. It was my job to focus on each step, on each moment, and to respond to each adversity along the way with clarity and resolve.

On my second trip through the Icefall, Chris Morris asked me how I was feeling about the expedition so far. "Sometimes," I replied, "I honestly feel like I'm just going through the motions. Sometimes I feel like I don't have a chance."

"Then you don't!" Chris shot back.

Those three words affected me like a punch in the gut.

After that, on rest days at Base Camp, I'd sit outside my tent and force myself to envision myself on the summit. In my mind, I'd touch the snow under my gloves and hear the Sherpa flags blowing in the wind. I'd taste the empty air, void of oxygen and humidity. I'd feel the tears welling up as I celebrated with my teammates. Suddenly I would be energized by the triumph I believed would come.

With each subsequent crossing, I began discovering little systems to shave precious minutes off my time. My partners had seen me rally on earlier expeditions, and thankfully they stuck by me. On the ladders, I learned to judge the distance between steps so that I could balance my crampon points over the rungs. I began to memorize the sequences of the zigzagging foot-wide snow bridges over dozens of crevasses. For the open crevasses where I had to jump, my teammates helped me by shouting out precisely when they were jumping and then landing, so I could gauge the distance and accurately copy their movements.

As we continued to make trips between camps, I concentrated on pushing fast through the easier sections and pacing myself through the tough parts. The minutes we saved added up to hours, and by my last trip up the Icefall, I had reduced my time from thirteen hours to less than five.

After two months on the mountain, we left on our final push for the summit. As I kicked up the face, my oxygen mask felt like it was suffocating me. Higher up, a lightning storm struck, stalling us for an hour as snow and

With a week left in the climbing season, my Everest team posed at Base Camp for a team shot before leaving for our last summit attempt. Out of twenty-one team members, nineteen of us reached the top–the most climbers from one team to reach the summit of Mount Everest together in a single day. Our flag reads "NFB 2001 Everest Expedition," honoring the participation of the National Federation of the Blind.

sleet blasted us sideways, built up on our down suits, and chilled us to the bone. Just below the summit, I inched my way across the Knife Edge Ridge, fully aware of the drop of 8,000 feet to my left and 12,000 feet to my right. I jokingly thought to myself that the good news was that it wouldn't really matter which side I fell off. The challenges were formidable, but in comparison to the Icefall, none felt anywhere near as daunting.

We had been climbing for twelve hours when Chris Morris wrapped his arms around me and said, "Erik, we're about to stand on top of the world!" When there was no place else to go, I reached down and touched my gloves to the hard snow, and listened to the Sherpa flags blowing in the wind. I could even taste the air—just as I had envisioned. Day after day I had worked myself to exhaustion; I had desperately fought against the uncertainty weighing me down like a mountain of doubt; a dozen times I had been on the verge of counting myself out. Even though my body now stood on the summit, my brain hadn't yet caught up. Choked with tears, I pulled out my radio and sputtered to the base camp crew, "We're on the top. I can't believe it! We're standing on top of the world!"

Paul

Understanding Your Adversity Quotient (AQ)

Your Adversity Quotient, or AQ, is a measure of how you respond to adversity of all kinds. People with a high AQ are resilient and resourceful, while people with a low AQ are easily overwhelmed. Your AQ is associated with a whole host of factors that influence success, including (but not limited to) your performance, resilience, engagement, innovation, attitude, energy, health, entrepreneurialism, and mental agility.

In 2002, my team and I formed the Global Resilience Project in order to build on the more than 1,500 studies that undergird the AQ theory. A collaboration of researchers worldwide, the

Global Resilience Project is dedicated to exploring and expanding the applications of AQ to better equip people for an adversity-rich world. We wanted to better understand exactly what the differences are between those who harness adversity and those who are consumed by it.

The research has revealed some compelling findings. We found that AQ can often be a more robust predictor of success than IQ. We've discovered, with mounting certainty, that when all other factors are held equal, high-AQ people rise to the top. They tend to outperform, outlast, outmaneuver, and outdo their low-AQ counterparts in essentially any endeavor. We discovered that leaders of industry often have dramatically higher AQs than the people working for them. This explains much of the gut burn of top leaders, and much of the stress experienced by workers. Leaders expect their people to demonstrate the same effectiveness under pressure that they themselves naturally possess.

Is your AQ something you are just born with? Or is it something you can consciously improve, once you are made aware of it? Fortunately, our research shows that this ability can be learned. We discovered not only that AQ can be measured, but also that it can be permanently improved. Hundreds of thousands of people have gone through our various AQ programs. The AQ of every group went up, and some individual AQs rose dramatically. After tracking some folks for more than a decade, we've found that once AQ goes up, it never drops back down. Measuring and improving AQ has been the focus of our work for many years, and as the science evolves, so do our AQ tools. To get a preview of your AQ, go to www.AQ-snapshot.com.

Posture is an apt analogy for AQ. Your posture may appear genetic, but chances are you hold yourself in a way that may be eerily similar to that of a parent or relative. Perhaps your entire family shares a distinctive posture—one all of your friends can instantly recognize from a distance, even if it is based on just a silhouette.

While posture is genetically influenced, it is largely determined by what you saw and subconsciously mimicked when you were little. Babies are profoundly observant. As an infant, you watched those around you stand, walk, sit, and engage in life, and you began to naturally model their postures. The more influential the person, the more you imitated him or her. By late childhood, you had formed your posture, which became so natural you could never imagine holding yourself any other way—unless someone came along, showed you some flaw in your current posture, gave you an enormously compelling reason to improve it, and coached you on exactly how to do so.

AQ is your posture with respect to adversity. It is mostly determined by what you saw and what you learned during your childhood. By watching the influential people in your life respond to adversity, you began to imitate their patterns, without consciously selecting those that would be best or worst.

The research on AQ and related response patterns dates back more than thirty-five years and was pioneered by Dr. Martin Seligman, of the University of Pennsylvania, and a cadre of other researchers worldwide. Generally this research indicates that at about age twelve, your AQ is highly formed. By age sixteen, or soon thereafter, it becomes hardwired for the rest of your life unless you are made aware of it and choose to change it. This book will help you recognize your AQ; offer compelling reasons to change it; and, by sharing the practices of the highest-AQ people, help you improve it.

Your CORE

Your CORE—which resides in the center of your Adversity Quotient—is the one thing you take with you into every battle. It ultimately determines whether you win or lose, both in the moment and over the long haul. Your CORE is the key to converting adversity into energy. Think of it as your portable adversity fuel cell. And the tougher the conditions, the more you may need its force.

You can use your CORE in any situation, for any challenge, setback, or opportunity. Top leaders and people in all walks of life use the CORE elements to respond better and faster to adverse events. Your CORE is composed of *Control*, *Ownership*, *Reach*, and *Endurance*.

Control (C)

It is impossible, and probably not even desirable, to have total control over our lives. But we all want some control over how we choose to spend our time, how we do our work, where we live, or what we eat. When it comes to adversity, the most important issue is not whether you are in complete control. What matters most is how much *influence you believe you have* in any given situation. When adversity strikes, *to what extent do you perceive you can influence whatever happens next?*

Some things you cannot change. You can't pick your genes or your family. You cannot go back in time and undo what has been done. You can't make life fair. But when life deals out a bad hand, high-AQ people don't sit there and bemoan their fate. They play their cards as skillfully as they can, looking for any opportunity they can turn to their advantage.

The Serenity Prayer, attributed in its lengthier entirety to Reinhold Niebuhr, gracefully clarifies the issue of *control* versus *influence:*

> *God grant me the serenity*
> *to accept the things I cannot change,*
> *courage to change the things I can,*
> *and wisdom to know the difference.*

The stirring beauty, strength, and truth of the Serenity Prayer are undeniable. So is the poem's utility as an inkblot test for AQ. Your AQ determines your perceived control. High-AQ people perceive they can always influence something, because even in dire circumstances they can at least influence their own response.

Picture two people facing the same setback. The low-AQ person reads the Serenity Prayer and interprets the adversity as something he must accept, because he cannot change it. The person with higher AQ, in the identical situation, will use his wisdom to see the difference between the aspects he cannot change and any number of factors he can influence for the better. This gives him the hope and energy to Take It On!

When Erik crossed the Khumbu Icefall, he could not change the random ice collapses, the terrible terrain, the immense distance, or his blindness. But he could influence his own mind—his focus and energy—so he could make it across, and do it again and again. Although it was a mental wrestling match, he had to see the Icefall as a piece of a puzzle that could be solved.

Imagine what might have happened if Erik had a lower AQ. Think of how differently he would have handled his blindness, how differently he would have defined his sphere of control. Everest has epic forces no one can control. The jet stream at the top can reach two hundred miles per hour. In fact, when Erik and his team were waiting at Camp Two for their push to the summit, they could hear the winds on top "roaring like a bad vacuum cleaner." They had to wait a week for the one or two days in May when winds calm down. Just as they were getting ready to make their summit push, it snowed for two weeks making the steep sides of the Lhotse Face unclimbable and forcing Erik's team back down the mountain, and through the Icefall an excruciating and potentially demoralizing eighth time. Anyone with a lower AQ would have quit, claiming that the mountain had turned him back. But

Erik focused on the things he could control, such as his fitness, supplies, strategy, and attitude, getting ready to give it another shot when the opportunity arose.

Perhaps this is why, of all four CORE dimensions, Control is the most robust in predicting health, and even longevity. A British study found that people in jobs who felt they had low control over how they did their work died on average five years earlier than those with high levels of perceived control. Today a similar study reveals the gap has nearly doubled, to 9.8 years. So people who perceive more control over how they do what they do may live nearly a full decade longer.

You can engage your CORE by asking yourself, "What facets of this situation can I potentially influence?" Even in dire circumstances there is always something you can control, starting with your point of view. When adversity hits, most people dramatically underestimate how much influence they really have. Becoming utterly obsessed with what you *can* influence opens worlds of possibilities. For an individual, that creates energy and engagement. For a business, it creates a competitive advantage.

Ownership (O)

The process of taking ownership involves recognizing that you can make a difference, then stepping up to do so. You do not have to shoulder the entire burden of a setback or challenge. But pointing fingers and blaming is a waste of time.

How likely are you to step forward to do something—anything, no matter how small—to improve a situation? Are you willing to take ownership of one piece of the problem to help make things better? Can you be the catalyst, the spark that ignites others and shifts the course of events in a positive direction? As you might guess, the people with higher AQs are more likely to step up and engage. Those with lower AQs are more likely to step back and disengage, probably because they are already overwhelmed!

In the business world, ownership is the one issue that brings tears to nearly every leader's eyes. Why? Because as the world speeds up and gets more demanding, chaotic, complex, and uncertain, people tend to focus more and more on what they *need* to do to survive, rather than what they *could* do to drive the next change, or innovate to the next level. When people don't step up, it's because they don't see how they could make a difference, or why they should bother. Key tasks are someone else's job. The less control people think they have, the less ownership they take, the more weary they become, and the less likely they are to step up the next time a challenge or opportunity arises. Lack of ownership can become a death spiral. Important priorities are not accomplished, so people become tired and demoralized, which prevents them from seeing positive ways to take ownership.

Ownership is one of the indisputable fibers of everyday greatness. Stepping up to help make things better not only elevates you, it elevates everyone around you. So when is the right time to step up? *When you least feel like it.* When you successfully force yourself to go the extra mile, you get an extra boost of energy and confidence. Ask yourself, "What can I do to affect this situation immediately and positively?" Don't worry about who caused it, or who is responsible for figuring out the ultimate solution. Don't ruin your precious momentum by waiting for others. Sometimes ownership is about going beyond the strict confines of your day job or responsibilities, even when you're extremely busy. Ownership is often about doing the right thing, even when it's not the required thing. Focus on *your* realm, *your* ownership, and watch how you inspire others to do the same.

Reach (R)

Adversity is like a black cloud that suddenly descends. At first we imagine that it extends in all directions, blanketing every aspect of our lives. But over time we realize this black cloud is not as enormous as we thought. In fact some parts of our life are not even affected by it. Other parts quickly return to normal. And with further adjustments, we create a "new normal" in the remaining areas. So exactly how big was this cloud, after all?

The perceived extent of the black cloud of adversity is called *reach*. Reach influences the burden you carry in life. If you allow it to do so, adversity will reach into all your thought processes, contaminating them with fear and dread, and immobilizing you with the belief that resistance is futile. The bigger and worse everything appears, the more suffocating life becomes, crushing you under its mass, making it difficult to keep your footing. But this doesn't have to happen. An optimistic and resilient outlook can cut your black cloud down to a manageable size so you can come up with strategies to harness it.

The flip side of reach is *containment*. The better you become at containing difficulties, the lighter you feel. The goal is to shrink the contamination, limit the downside, and grow the upside, which unleashes newfound energy and possibilities.

Do you know anyone who suffers from emotional oil spills? You know, the kind of person whose entire day is ruined when one thing goes wrong, or whose entire project is destroyed by one minor mistake. Psychologists call this reaction to adversity *catastrophizing*. People with low AQs are more likely to perceive a setback as massive and all consuming. They say, "We just lost our biggest customer, we're ruined!" or, "I'm flunking out of school!" People with high AQs contain the fallout, not letting it become any bigger than necessary. They say, "That was a tough meeting," or, "Gee, I got disappointing grades this quarter."

Erik has to focus on reach and containment every time he climbs. On Everest, as in life, one of the greatest challenges is not letting fear, doubt, and uncertainty gnaw at your resolve. These are the forces that make up much of the lore of the mountain. The day before Erik's ascent from Camp Two to Camp Three, a twenty-year-old man tripped and fell down the Lhotse Face—that exceptionally steep ice slope. He spent the better part of the waning day lying there in the snow, abandoned for dead, before another climber was able to save him. Then, on the day before Erik's push to the summit, a Swiss man clipped his anchor onto the wrong rope, fell, and died. If Erik had let these events take root and spread in his psyche, they could easily have compromised or even ended his climb. But he contained the influence of these events and used them as powerful reminders to stay absolutely focused all the way to the top.

Limit the scope and fallout of your adversity by asking yourself:

▸ How can I contain this adversity?
▸ How can I minimize the downside?
▸ What can I do to optimize the potential upside?

The higher your AQ, the more possibilities you'll perceive in even the most tragic situations. This does not mean you should be a "disengaged" optimist, the kind of person who is blissfully unaware of harsh reality and does little to influence the outcome of adversity. When Erik assembles a climbing team, he absolutely avoids the dreamy optimists. They're dangerous. The idea is to be an "engaged" optimist, the kind of person who has the capacity to hope for the best that is possible, as well as the ability to be brutally realistic about the worst that could happen. People with high AQs are hopeful that their relentless, strategically focused efforts will increase the chance that things will turn out better over time. They prepare for the worst, but expect the best.

Endurance (E)

The final dimension of CORE has to do with time, or duration. The key question: *How long do you predict this adversity will last?* Your answer will either fill you with dread, or fill you with hope. People with low AQs tend to see setbacks as long-term, even permanent. Change becomes a grueling, drawn-out process, and they feel crushed under its hulk. People with high AQs remain hopeful that the adversity will not endure that long. Sometimes they break a challenge down into manageable pieces that pass relatively quickly. They see change as temporary, something they can work through and be energized by.

Although physical endurance may come into play, the issue here is your emotional fortitude in light of how long you think your challenge will endure. Ask yourself, "How can I get through this as quickly as possible?" Use this question to dispel the assumption that a specific adversity has to drag on and on.

Erik

Raising Your Adversity Quotient

When you are faced with adversity—the rejection letter arrived, your partner is stressing you out, your job was eliminated, your MRI results were not good—these are the times when you need your Adversity Quotient to be functioning at its best. These are also the times when, at least at first, you are most likely to want to pull the covers over your head. Following are four techniques you can use to keep moving in a positive direction: Celebrating Stepping-Stones, the Summit Game, the Failure Fantasy, and Positive Pessimism.

Celebrating Stepping-Stones

When I took on Mount Everest, I knew that the three months of relentless effort would take its toll. We didn't just climb the mountain once; we went up and down the mountain multiple times to supply the higher camps, making repeated crossings through the Khumbu Icefall. We waited out countless storms, including one that sent us scrambling as it shredded our tents. The local, unrefrigerated Sherpa food continually made us sick with dysentery.

Sometimes thinking about the expedition as a whole was just too overwhelming. To stay focused and sane, I broke the expedition into legs and created mini-finish lines. I would concentrate on just getting to the next camp, where I could rest and refuel. During long days, my teammates would help me envision the next rest stop by saying things like "three hundred yards above us, we'll rest at the top of the Geneva Spur." The strategy was to envision the next finish line, and then work to get there. You, too, can create your own stepping-stones when the task you face is particularly daunting.

The Summit Game

My running partner, Gavin Attwood, first taught me the Summit Game when I was training for Mount Everest. Daily, we'd run uphill on a steep rocky trail behind my house, attached together by a bungee cord so I could feel his direction in front of me. During the most brutal uphill push, when my lungs were bursting and I didn't know how I could keep going, he taught me to envision myself at the finish line with all the elation of that moment—and I would find the strength to keep going.

I used this technique on Everest, often sitting outside my base camp tent, conjuring up a mental image of the summit. I used it again above the

Hillary Step at 28,900 feet, with only forty minutes to go. I had been counting my breaths between steps. They went from three to five to six breaths, and I was starting to hit a brick wall. But I kept envisioning myself and my team standing on top, and, suddenly, I would have the energy to take another step. It was like I had been given a loan just when I needed it most—and the best part was that I never had to pay it back.

Since then, I've used this technique many times when hammered by wind, ravaged by fatigue, and pierced by cold, and it has never failed. Sometimes, when I'm feeling wasted and discouraged, the transformation is so powerful that I instantly feel my eyes filling with tears of joy in anticipation of the summit.

Practicing the Summit Game definitely makes the technique more effective. The root of this exercise, however, is a strong belief in your outcome, and that doesn't always come easily. I guess you could say you have to believe yourself forward.

Paul calls this principle Energy Lending. It relates back to the Endurance element of his CORE strategy, and his research shows it has a basis in science. Imagining an exhilarating event, such as winning, achieving your goal, or summiting a mountain, can release the same neuropeptides in the body that the actual event would release. The greater your imagination and immersion in the fantasy, the more energy and positive chemistry you will enjoy.

The Failure Fantasy

The inverse of the Summit Game is the Failure Fantasy. Although positive motivation works best, I think fear and pain can also be good motivators, and they are often underrated. Sometimes I use the Failure Fantasy for motivation before I head out for a long summit day. I think about the implications of failure, and I use them as fuel when I'm tired, in pain, and have been on my feet for twelve hours. Under these circumstances, failure is simply not an option. I try to connect with the disappointment and anguish that failure would bring. I don't use the threat of not succeeding to push myself unsafely, but it does help me to do my absolute best and to strive to reach my greatest potential. I know that the pain of falling short will far outweigh the physical pain and mental uncertainty I'm experiencing in the immense effort to win.

As it turns out, the Failure Fantasy is also substantiated by Paul's CORE research. At first the reach of a particular adversity may seem so pervasive that it appears insurmountable. But allowing the awful scenario of failure to scroll across your internal movie screen forces you to think through all the consequences, and to experience the feelings of frustration, regret, and embarrassment associated with failure. If the mental dress rehearsal is excruciating enough, the thought of having to live through the failure may be just the kick-start you need to regroup and redouble your efforts.

I first started using the Failure Fantasy as a teenager, just after losing my sight. Sitting in the cafeteria, I'd think about my life as a blind person. My fear was that if I didn't face the facts, embrace what had happened, and take steps to climb my way out, I was going to end up just listening to life go by as a spectator, never experiencing life as a participant. This fear turned out to be just the push I needed to try rock climbing when the chance presented itself.

I think others who have been hurt, physically or emotionally, can use their fear of inaction as a motivator. They can imagine what their life will be like if they cannot adequately face what has happened to them. Maybe they contemplate what it would be like never to have a family or a job, never to complete a lifelong dream or experience anything fulfilling. At that moment, there comes a tipping point when the fear and pain of doing nothing outweighs the fear and pain of taking a first step.

Positive Pessimism

My friend and climbing partner, Chris Morris, is known for a little trick he uses to deal with hardship. He calls it "positive pessimism." We'll be sitting out in a raging storm. We've gone a month without showers. The wind is

I navigated through the treacherous Khumbu Icefall ten times. The Icefall is a blind person's worst nightmare, with no two steps ever the same. My first trip through was the hardest day of my life in the mountains, way too slow at thirteen hours and dramatically increasing my chances of getting hit by falling ice. If I couldn't find a way to get through it in half the time, I knew I'd need to go down.

driving snow directly into our faces, and I'm wondering what insanity led me to this nightmare in the first place. That's when Chris will look up with a big cheesy smile on his face and say, "Sure is cold out here . . . but at least it's windy." Another time, we had been moving through the cold for ten hours, and we were all wasted. Chris turned to our team and said, "Boys, we sure have been climbing a long way . . . but at least we're lost." In the Khumbu Icefall, as Chris was halfway across his first ladder over a giant crevasse, he came out with the classic: "This ladder may be rickety . . . but at least it's swingin' in the breeze."

Positive pessimism is a humorous way to take the edge off your current problems. If you can throw out a positive pessimism when you're really hurting, it helps you maintain some control over your predicament by giving you a healthy perspective. Once I overheard a guy who was hiking with me in Colorado, and struggling to keep up the pace, say from behind me, "I may be fat . . . but at least I'm old." Embracing the gravity of your situation with humor and humility speaks loudly about your character and helps those around you to stay cheerful. It's like saying, "This may be a grim situation, and I know we're all suffering, but we can get through it."

On Aconcagua, I had just struggled to the 22,841-foot summit. I was barely hanging in there and worried about falling on the long descent. Chris gave me a big hug and croaked, "Big E, you may be blind . . . but at least you're slow!" Oddly, his statement made me feel that Chris believed in me, and that we would be okay. In fact, as fatigued as I was, I grinned and shot back, "Chris, you're not the nicest guy in the world . . . but at least you're stupid."

I've seen people use positive pessimism in all aspects of life. How about "I'm going into a three-hour meeting . . . but at least I didn't have time to eat lunch," or "We may not have gotten the account . . . but at least our stock price went down." At home, try this one: "Honey, we may be on a really tight budget . . . but at least our heating bill doubled." Or "We may be moving into a smaller house . . . but at least your mother is coming to live with us."

With a week to go until this book was due at the publisher, I went into my computer file and found that the entire chapter I had been writing was deleted. My first reaction was to do something violent, but then I thought of my good friend Chris Morris and said to myself, "I may have lost the chapter . . . but at least I'll be up for the next three nights rewriting it."

⟋	Paul

Building Your CORE

We all have plenty of opportunities to engage with inner and outer adversity. Your approach to adversity—your CORE—determines how much you benefit from a setback and how soon you rebound. Strengthening your CORE will equip you with the capacity to perform your own brand of alchemy, turning challenges into opportunities, and opportunities into victories. A devastating tornado becomes an opportunity to rebuild, start fresh, and reconnect with what matters most. A downturn in the market is an opportunity to refocus, retrench, and reinvest so you come out on the upswing better and faster than your competitors. A brutal divorce is an opportunity for introspection, growth, and self-improvement. A failed stint at school becomes the galvanizing event for doing your best going forward. A bankruptcy clears the decks to reinvent your life. Some people are even able to look back and see cancer as a gift, Lance Armstrong for example. Ask people who have prevailed over adversity if, given the choice, they would do it all over again, and many say "yes."

Ask for Feedback

I've found the most practical way to build your CORE is through heightened awareness, with feedback from multiple sources that provides a 360-degree, or panoramic, perspective. This process shines a light on your blind spots, so you can grow stronger. It is especially helpful for leaders, whose behavior can affect the lives of hundreds of people.

To get started, list those people who have had a long-standing opportunity to see you respond to life's unexpected turns, day in and day out. Try to include some people from work and some from outside of work. You are looking for an honest assessment, so don't pick people who might have something to lose from telling you the truth.

To enlist their help, you might say, "I have been reading this book about how people respond to adversity, and I realized it is something I'd like to do better." If necessary, define what you mean by adversity. You can ask for written or verbal responses, whichever will give you the most useful feedback.

Following are some useful questions you can use to evaluate your CORE skills. Be sure to ask for illustrations for each answer. Specific examples about what people have observed are always more helpful than general impressions.

- ► On a scale of one to ten (ten being the highest), how effectively do you think I respond to adversity, in general?
- ► Am I more effective with certain types of adversity than others?
- ► Are there certain times when I deal better with adversity than others?
- ► What is the most positive example you can recall of how I dealt with adversity? How about the most negative?
- ► When adversity strikes, do I tend more toward helplessness, or toward being in control?
- ► When something goes wrong, how likely would it be for me to step up to do something to make the situation better?
- ► Do you think I tend to let adversity spill over into everything else?
- ► In your experience, is my attitude toward adversity closer to "this will quickly pass" or "this will last forever!"?

- ► What do you like best about the way I handle adversity? What do you dislike?
- ► If you were coaching me on how to handle adversity more effectively, what is the one thing you'd recommend I do more, less, or differently?

Your CORE Awareness

"What's my CORE?" can become your instant pulse check when difficulties strike. The simplest but most profound way to build your CORE is to pay keen attention to what thoughts, words, and emotions spark inside of you the moment you face any kind of adversity. To perform a CORE status check, ask yourself the following questions:

Control (C) How much influence do I have over this situation?
Ownership (O) To what extent am I stepping up to make things better?
Reach (R) How big am I letting this become?
Endurance (E) To what extent am I letting this drag on?

I am always impressed by the stories people tell me, long after attending an Adversity Advantage program, about how tuning into their CORE made a world of difference for them. Whether in your relationships, job, health, or other pursuits, build your CORE each time a challenge arises in your path.

Recognize CORE Elements in Action

Another way to build your CORE is through heightened awareness of CORE elements in action around you. Everywhere you go—in every conversation you hear, movie you watch, book you read, newscast you hear, or presentation you enjoy—listen for the CORE elements.

Immediately you'll hear facets of Control as people say, "There's nothing we can do about this now. It's too late." Or "We can do this. We've tackled worse before."

You'll see people step up, or step back, demonstrating the vital role Ownership plays in getting anything done and any problem resolved. You'll hear it when people make statements like "Well, I hope they figure out something," versus "I don't know all the answers, but I promise to get some of them for you right away."

You'll recognize the Reach in people's responses when they utter classics such as "This is a complete disaster. We're doomed!" Or "If we act quickly, we can more than recover!"

You will be inspired, or demoralized, by people's different views of Endurance when they say things like "We'll never get out of *this* one." Or "We are just going through a tough phase. It won't last long."

Once you start looking for CORE elements, you'll recognize them everywhere. You're looking for clues to the best possible way to handle adversity. When you see someone putting a CORE element to good use, make a mental note to do the same yourself. Soon you'll have a reservoir of proven techniques to draw upon when you need them.

Employ the CORE Strategy

Hundreds of corporate employees and thousands of individuals have come to PEAK Learning requesting our guidance in creating disaster response plans, executing strategic plans, dealing with market fluctuations, optimizing a particular opportunity, or simply working through a difficult situation. The CORE Strategy is the tool we teach people to use in order to maximize the potential advantage of any specific adversity—or, for organizations, to respond better and faster than their competition. This exercise will help you engage your CORE (and the COREs of others) and to turn adversity to your advantage better and faster than you currently do.

Take out some blank paper and write down your Summit Challenge. (We ask participants to begin with a particularly difficult challenge or goal, personal or professional, organizational or private.) Now read the questions below and write down your answers. The questions can be asked of an individual or a group. Note: The CORE Strategy generates a lot of ideas, but don't judge them as you come up with them. Just list them. The scrutiny comes later.

Questions about Control (C)
- What is clearly beyond your control?
- What factors can you potentially influence?
- Of the things you could potentially influence in this situation, which two are the most important?

Questions about Ownership (O)
- Where and how can you step up to make the most immediate positive difference in this situation?

Questions about Reach (R)
- What is the worst-case scenario?
- What is the best thing that could possibly happen, however unlikely?
- What actions can you take to minimize the potential downside of this situation?
- What actions can you take to maximize the potential upside of this situation? (Note: As soon as you begin working on building the upside of a given adversity, chances are you are already way ahead of everyone else!)

Questions about Endurance (E)

▶ What do you want life to be like on the other side of this adversity (or living with this adversity)? Describe it in detail.

▶ What other actions can you take to get there as quickly and completely as possible?

The brain is constantly forging new neural pathways. With energy, focus, and effort we can build new connections and create new patterns of thinking and behaving. The purpose of these questions is to help you begin to shake free of the old assumptions that hold your CORE pattern in place. Now you'll have both new approaches to old problems, and also a new way to respond to future setbacks.

The CORE Strategy questions are simple, and they work. They can be used in any order, with anyone, in any situation to become more resilient and effective. As you apply each question to your Summit Adversity, it should quickly convert into a vital energy source for fueling your success with your Summit Challenge.

Create a CORE Action Plan

The final step in the CORE Strategy is to devise a specific action plan so you can gain traction immediately. Post the entire list of potential actions, which you derived from the CORE Strategy, in plain view.

▶ Pick what you are going to do first.

▶ Give yourself a deadline. By when will this be accomplished?

▶ Consider the logistics. How are you going to do it?

▶ Prepare for any difficulties. What is the most likely obstacle, and how will you deal with it?

▶ What is Plan B, in the event Plan A fails or falls short?

When there are several parties involved, it is best to record your answers. You will know you succeeded when all parties have a clear sense of what they are to do, by when, and how. No one should leave empty-handed.

Imagine the possibilities. As you are strategizing steps toward life on the other side of a given difficulty, others are still reeling. As you generate hope, others are mired in despair. Your energy ramps up while others remain demoralized. This puts you in the ideal position to win personally, and hopefully to help others in your life to engage their COREs, so they can win, too.

Erik

Ernest Shackleton

In my opinion, there is no better example of thriving through adversity than the survival story of my hero, Sir Ernest Shackleton. While the story has been told many times, as a popular way to teach leadership and teamwork, I have always looked at it differently.

To me, the hardships and suffering Shackleton and the crew of the *Endurance* faced when they became stranded near Antarctica defy comprehension. For nearly two years, and through the most brutal conditions known to man, Shackleton doggedly hung on to a belief that he could influence his situation and, by doing so, he kept his men motivated, confident, and, most important, alive.

Shackleton's original goal was to become the first to make a full traverse of Antarctica. His ship left the island of South Georgia in early December 1914, passed the South Sandwich Islands, and plowed through a thousand miles of ice-encrusted waters. A month into the voyage, however, the *Endurance* experienced an unexpected deep freeze and became lodged in a polar ice pack. They were just one day from their destination at

Vahsel Bay on the Antarctic continent. Still, Shackleton and his crew were stranded more than twelve hundred miles from the closest settlement, and they had only each other to rely on for survival.

In the months that followed, they could do little to improve their situation; they could only wait until the spring thaw. Several times they thought they'd be set free, only to have their hopes dashed. For ten months the moving ice dragged their ship until it was ultimately crushed. They salvaged only enough items necessary for survival, plus a banjo and personal journals for the twenty-seven members of the crew. Although they spent five more months camped on the moving ice in flimsy tents and had to ration their meager food, they remained optimistic and energetic. Often they played soccer, performed music, and danced on the empty ice floes.

Finally, as the ice began to break, the crew set sail in three small lifeboats with the hope of coming into contact with the whaling ships along the northern tip of the continent. Instead the currents took them to Elephant Island, a barren and isolated land raked by intense storms. With no hope of rescue and knowing his men couldn't survive for long, Shackleton took five men and sailed eight hundred miles in a twenty-two-foot wooden lifeboat, over the open ocean and through the roughest weather on earth. Seventeen days later, they fortuitously reached the island of South Georgia, where they had begun.

Coming ashore, they were struck with a final terrible blow. They had landed on the opposite, uninhabited side of the island. To reach the one settlement, they would have to trek a week over rugged, glaciated mountains with no climbing equipment, a journey considered impossible even with the best gear of the day. For most people this final obstacle alone would have been enough to bring defeat, but to Shackleton it was simply another adversity he had to attack. Starving, frostbitten, and wearing rags, Shackleton and two of his men reached the tiny whaling station, and twenty-two months after starting their voyage, Shackleton returned in person for his men left behind on Elephant Island. The crew was emaciated but, amazingly, all were alive. Shackleton hadn't lost a single man.

What seems the most remarkable to me is that throughout the two-year ordeal, although the adversity must have felt massive and the endurance never-ending, Shackleton and his men never gave up control over their destiny. They continued to demonstrate intense loyalty to each other and responsibility for keeping the team alive. A crew member, Frank Hurley, later wrote, "I always found Shackleton rising to his best and inspiring confidence when things were at their blackest."

In my opinion, although Shackleton failed at his original objective, he succeeded at something even more unimaginable. In the face of unbelievably low odds, he infused in his men the belief that they had the capacity to prevail. As Shackleton put it, "By endurance, we conquer."

If Shackleton's crew had so much power to affect the course of their lives under such dire conditions, it begs the question: How much control do we have over our affairs in our everyday lives, and how much of that power do we choose to assert—or relinquish? Too many people go through life like a pinball, constantly being directed by circumstances and events but never forging a deliberate path through life's perils.

I've learned that every time I face a challenge on the mountain or in life, I can gain some control over my fate by focusing on what I can influence, taking action to make the best of tough situations, minimizing the potential downside and maximizing the upside, plus taking the point of view that the suffering has an endpoint, and I can endure until that point is reached. I hope you will now employ the same strategies that drove Shackleton's crew to persevere, and propelled me to the top of Mount Everest.

Pioneer Possibilities

MOUNT ELBRUS

Base Camp: 9,000 feet

Summit: 18,510 feet

Mount Elbrus, located in Russia, is the tallest peak in Europe.

I dream of things that never were and say, "Why not?"

–GEORGE BERNARD SHAW

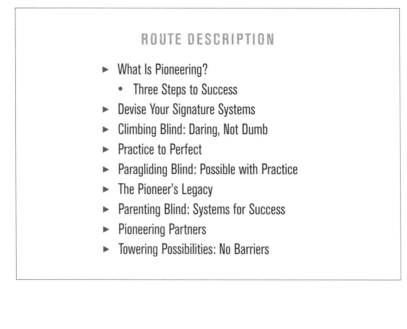

ROUTE DESCRIPTION

- ▶ What Is Pioneering?
  - • Three Steps to Success
- ▶ Devise Your Signature Systems
- ▶ Climbing Blind: Daring, Not Dumb
- ▶ Practice to Perfect
- ▶ Paragliding Blind: Possible with Practice
- ▶ The Pioneer's Legacy
- ▶ Parenting Blind: Systems for Success
- ▶ Pioneering Partners
- ▶ Towering Possibilities: No Barriers

Erik

When we reach out and try to be innovative in our lives, we usually smack up against a wall of adversity. Conversely, when we experience a big-time challenge, it can propel us toward a creative solution. Innovation and adversity can be seen as partners, exchanging the lead in a never-ending dance. That relationship was made clear to me when I decided to climb up and ski down the tallest peak in Europe, Mount Elbrus.

I had already climbed Everest—11,000 feet higher and a whole lot tougher. I suppose my team and I could have approached Mount Elbrus as just another of the Seven Summits to check off the scorecard, but instead my climbing partner, Eric Alexander, and I asked each other, "How do we stretch ourselves to make this expedition even more exciting and meaningful?"

We decided the most compelling challenge would be not only to ascend by the seldom climbed northern route, but to ski nearly 10,000 feet from the summit to Base Camp. No blind person had ever skied a major world peak. The idea was breathtaking. Then the questions started.

Climbing through steep snow, ice, and rock with twenty extra pounds of ski gear, and then skiing back down through rugged, unforgiving terrain introduced an entirely new set of problems. Ironically, that was actually part of the appeal—to create a plan, work through a process rife with difficulties, and see whether it could be done. The idea of skiing down Elbrus after an arduous climb, feeling the wind in my face and the speed beneath my feet, was exhilarating. What a wild ride that would be! Equally intriguing was the idea that we could nudge other people to rethink what's possible.

Eric and I would need to employ our ingenuity to overcome some major hurdles. Sometimes you can meet a challenge by applying known methods in new ways. Other times an entirely new approach may be required. To succeed at our quest, we would have to invent new systems to communicate, navigate, and function as one unit.

Eric Alexander guided me as we skied 10,000 vertical feet from the summit to Base Camp on Mount Elbrus. Lower on the mountain, the terrain opened up and we had fun making powder eights in the snow.

Eric and I trained for an entire year, devising new ways to communicate while speeding down a mountain together with only one ski length between us. Traditionally, blind skiers have been coached from behind. But I now know this system is precisely wrong because the skier is forced to react suddenly.

Instead, we devised a system of coaching from the front. This lets me hear verbal cues that both describe the turn and provide a sense of direction. Every word out of Eric's mouth had to translate into a precise and predictable action on my part.

Ski turns have three sequential steps—getting the skis up on edges to initiate the turn, facing straight down the fall line, and bringing the skis around for the finish. So Eric learned to call out turns in three syllables, "Turn . . . a . . . left! Turn . . . a . . . right!" With each syllable, I'd know exactly where I needed to be in the maneuver. He could also elongate or shorten the call to indicate what size turn to make. A gradual turn would sound like, "Tuuuuuuuurn aaaaaaaa leeeeeeeeft." On a severe angle where I had to get my skis around quickly, he'd drop the middle syllable and yell, "Hard left!"

One of the exciting—actually, terrifying—aspects of skiing blind is that I'm only able to react to variables like sudden drops as I feel them under my skis. So to ease the transitions, Eric learned to call, "Steeper!" or "Flatter!" In the narrower sections, where we wanted to maintain our speed, Eric could extend a pole to me, enabling me to stay in sync with him on each turn. Eric and I even practiced with a new high-tech radio that let us communicate the turns when gale-force winds kicked in.

High speed, combined with my lack of sight, leaves no room for error. My worst nightmare was tumbling into oblivion or hitting a rock at twenty miles per hour. We practiced relentlessly to get the new systems hardwired so we could count on them working in any conditions.

When the day of our summit push finally arrived, it took everything I had to make it to the top. I was completely spent, and my legs were rubbery from the weight of the extra gear. I turned to Eric and admitted, "I don't know if I can do this." He was silent for a minute, and then I felt the sting of his gloved hand smack me on the side of the head.

"We trained for a year," he said, clearly annoyed. "We're skiing this mountain!"

So I wobbled up to my feet, clicked into my skis, and—rubbery legs and all—careened down the ridge. The fear inspired by hanging from my fingertips high up on a rock face was nothing compared to hurtling blind down a high-altitude peak. The conditions would go instantly from deep powder to rock-hard snow, frozen into waves by the wind. Although Eric did his best to avoid drop-offs, I went over a few small ones, and when you can't see the landing, even a second of being airborne is unnerving. After every five jostling turns, I'd hang over my ski poles, gasping for air.

On the long traversing sections, Eric took my pole and we skied side by side, our skis only six inches apart. Later he stayed right behind me, navigating us down icy gullies, past cliff bands, and around rocks. When the afternoon winds kicked up, we had our radios ready to go.

Later in the descent, Eric and I became immersed in a whiteout. In these conditions, it's hard for sighted folks to distinguish the ground from the sky; everything loses its contrast. Eric didn't skip a beat as he switched to calling turns from behind me, but later he admitted he had used the bright red contrast of my jacket several times to tell him where the drop-offs were. Some things are better learned after the experience.

When we were 3,000 feet above camp, with the most difficult sections behind us and more oxygen to breathe, Eric said, "It's wide open in front of you—nothing to hit even if you tried." So I tucked my body and leaned forward. The strength in my legs rebounded as I picked up speed. With the wind in my face and the blood pulsing in my ears, I sensed the soft powder flying by. It was easy to imagine that Eric and I had lifted up off the earth and were skiing through the clouds.

Almost a year later we learned that our system of verbal ski commands was actually not so novel; it was almost the same system the Blue Angels use to fly their F/A-18 Hornets in their renowned six-jet Delta Formation, often with only twenty-four inches between wingtips. In hindsight, I can say that if it worked for them, it was going to work for us. In fact, at a few points on the run, I felt like my descent was approaching the speed of sound.

Some people have told me that the days of pioneering are over, that the great discoveries on earth have already been made, but this outlook is horribly limited. The literal definition of *discover* is "to unveil." Imagine how much of science, technology, and human potential is still veiled by darkness. It is only by attacking our personal challenges with a pioneering spirit that we can drive our own lives forward, and even shape the destiny of our organizations, our communities, and society at large.

Being a pioneer in the modern world doesn't necessarily mean undertaking scary first ascents, rocketing to Mars, or discovering the cure for cancer. But it does mean being motivated more from within, rather than by other people's expectations, which have a slippery way of turning into barriers. In the face of great challenges, pioneering means asking the question: How do I do what I want to do with the resources I have? The answer probably involves reaching much further than what is comfortable.

Pioneers take other people's beliefs about what is possible and shatter them into a million pieces. The exciting part is that each time those perceptions are rebuilt, they get bigger and more expansive. With an innovative and gutsy approach to challenges, each of us has a rare chance to blast through barriers and to expand opportunities for those who come after us.

Paul

What Is Pioneering?

How many times in your life has someone told you that something you wanted to do was impossible? Have your associates, friends, and loved ones ever tried to "talk some sense" into you when you got some "harebrained scheme" to try something new, or to take a risk they perceived as foolish? What if they were caring . . . but wrong? What if that thing you've always dreamt of doing is possible? How would it feel to be the one who made it happen? And what if, by making the impossible possible, you opened a whole new world of opportunities for yourself, your organization, and the people around you? Anyone would find that exciting.

If necessity is the mother of invention, then adversity is the father of innovation. Both necessity and adversity force us to be resourceful. Our natural human ingenuity can come out in every arena. How many broken-down cars have limped to a service station on a makeshift repair of duct tape, baling wire, or chewing gum? How many restaurants have invented "specials" when they ran out of the standard menu choices? Think of all the organizations that live or die by their ability to pivot with a new, ingenious idea. How many enterprises have engineered major breakthroughs when faced with a supply shortage, too much inventory, or the prospect of going bankrupt? How many entrepreneurs pioneered new ways to balance family and work demands? How many times have *you* found a way when there was no way?

Whenever a pioneer creates a groundbreaking system, or does anything new of any real consequence, he or she must work through a significant amount of adversity. I call using ingenuity and tenacity to do something different and better "possibility pioneering." Every day, parents, teachers, and professionals find new ways to do the impossible in the face of real deadlines, dilemmas, and limitations. To succeed, you must ask yourself: "How do I do what I need to do with the resources I have (or can build around me)?" The answer might require you to reach beyond what you thought possible.

Three Steps to Success

This chapter is about *creating systems* and *developing new ways to accomplish tasks*. How can you make the undoable doable, and pioneer new possibilities so you continue to grow and flourish? Following is a simple, three-step process for doing exactly that:

Step 1: Select a worthy challenge. It should stretch you in new ways and represent new possibilities. It should be something that involves some kind of risk or resistance, and just the idea of completing it should make you tingle with excitement. You already have your Summit Challenge, so you can go directly to the next step!

Step 2: Engineer the Signature Systems that will be the key to your success. You will need a personalized, customized, original way to do what it is you want to do. Like your signature, your systems become uniquely yours, and people will associate them with you once they see them implemented. Ordinarily you would begin with the typical action plan: setting specific, realistic, achievable, and measurable steps that you can achieve in a timely manner. This is excellent for everyday goals, but not gutsy enough for your Summit Challenge.

Step 3: Practice to perfect. Refine your new systems so they work consistently, especially when it counts the most. While others are still managing the downside, you will be generating and perfecting an upside.

When it comes to harnessing adversity and living at the top of the Adversity Continuum, complacency is your enemy; innovation is your friend. Over the course of your life and career, has your perception of what's possible grown, or shrunk? Compared to years past, do you believe more, or less, is really possible? Do you spend most of your time doing what's tried and true, or do you continually invent new ways to get things done? How do you respond when someone comes to you with the question, "What if . . . ?"

Every organization must innovate to survive. The relationship between adversity and innovation was substantiated through comprehensive research by Dr. Gideon Markman at the University of Georgia, who discovered that those people who had the highest AQs (those who responded to adversity most effectively) generated the most innovation. Those with the lowest AQs tended to innovate the least. Since Markman's study, my team and I have observed the same dynamic time and time again. We see non-profit organizations embark on new fund-raising approaches when faced with slashed budgets. We see sales teams reassemble the value package they bring to clients when faced with a crumbling economy. We see entire workforces step up to new challenges they must take on in order to stay alive, let alone win. In fact, we constantly rediscover that, without adversity, many possibilities would remain, well, impossible.

Adversity is the parent of our possibilities. At work, when budgets get tightened and the goals raised, what do *you* do? Do you throw up your hands and declare, "This is *impossible!*" Or do you work on finding a way to make the impossible possible? Guess which approach gets you promoted? When there are competing, important demands, and there is "simply no way" to get it all done, how do you respond? Do you get stymied and stressed, or do you reassemble the pieces in a way that makes it all happen, even better than it otherwise would? When you get a grim diagnosis, when you are faced with the hardships of raising your children by yourself, when the employee you most rely on leaves for another opportunity, do you succumb to your fate? Or do you focus your best energies on rallying around your Summit Challenge, devising and perfecting your Signature Systems to make the impossible possible?

This is where the creative juices can really kick in. The act of pioneering possibilities will most likely mean that you will need to invent new ways of doing something, ways that are customized to your style or needs. The good news is you don't have to be a creative genius to play at this game. If, as in the case of your Summit Challenge, your goal is worthy and you want it badly enough, solutions will emerge.

Devise Your Signature Systems

To conquer your Summit Challenge, you will need an approach that is yours alone, to suit your unique style, needs, and circumstances. In time others may adapt your Signature Systems to suit their circumstances, too.

Begin by writing down all of the possible solutions that come into your mind. It's easiest to begin with resources you already have, but a brilliant solution may require new resources. It's also easiest to begin with the strengths you already have, but as we have seen, you can develop new strengths if necessary, or bring people onto your team who will complement your strengths.

To help generate solutions, ask yourself:

▶ How would the most creative person I know solve this challenge?

▶ How would an expert approach this?

▶ What other creative solutions or existing systems could I modify or adapt?

After you have a list of possibilities, decide which one is most likely to work. Choose a solution that will hold your attention and interest while you practice and refine it. The best solutions are usually the simplest . . . but it's not always easy to create something simple! The most effective solution is elegant in its simplicity, causes a minimum of hassles, and is not burdened by complexity, which only creates more opportunities for things to go wrong.

Erik

Climbing Blind: Daring, Not Dumb

I don't see myself as a crazy Evel Knievel being shot across the Snake River Canyon in a rocket. I don't take massive amounts of risk, and I do hope to live through my adventures. Being blind is one thing, but blind and stupid could be fatal. I take calculated risks, not crazy ones. I see myself more as a problem solver who looks at challenges others perceive as improbable, and who tries to figure out a way forward.

A blind person gets pretty good at developing Signature Systems that help him or her accomplish tasks a sighted person takes for granted. I match my socks by placing safety pins on the toe if they're black, on the heel if they're blue, and on the top if they're brown. I can tell how big a room is by the echo—by the way sound vibrations bounce off the walls and ceiling. When I was in college, I invented my most ingenious system. Girls would sometimes tell me, "I feel so comfortable with you. I know you're not judging me by my surface beauty, but by my inner beauty." What they didn't know about was my secret handshake. Each time one of my male friends approached, the specific way he'd shake my hand would tell me exactly what she looked like.

On a big mountain or vertical face, developing and honing new strategies are essential. Those Signature Systems make your team safer, more productive, and more efficient, and many times they are the difference between success and disaster. For example, there are a half dozen different knots to be tied, often while wearing thick gloves, each used in a different circumstance. There's a specific way to put on crampons; buckled incorrectly, a loose strap could trip you and send you cartwheeling down the mountain. Choosing the right layering system at midnight when you are squeezed into a tent the size of a coffin determines whether you'll become hypothermic in your twentieth hour on the go. Organizing your pack so you can easily get to the most important gear first will help you avoid frostbite.

So often in our daily lives, there is a way, if only we can create it. Sometimes there's a book to read, a procedure in place, or a manual to follow. But often we're on our own. When we have to engineer our own strategies, tools, and systems from the ground up, that's where adventure lies.

When I thought about ice climbing—climbing frozen waterfalls—many experts told me that it wasn't a smart idea. "It's not like rock climbing," one person said. "Ice is unstable. You have big, heavy, sharp metal tools in your hands and you have to know exactly where to strike the face. If you swing your tool in the wrong spot, you'll knock down a giant chunk of ice, the size of a refrigerator. It will come down and crush you, or even worse, your partner." That seemed pretty bad to me.

I knew I couldn't ascend like sighted climbers, by swinging at the solid blue ice and not at the rotten white ice. So by trial and error, I figured out how to use my hearing instead of my sight. I learned to use my ice tools as extensions of my hands, feeling through their tips. When I find a weak spot in the ice or a concave dish above a bulge, I tap one tool, feeling the vibration through the ice and listening for the auditory pitch of the tap. If I hear a "dong!" like the sound of ringing a big hollow bell, that means big ice coming down on top of me; don't swing there! If I hear a tinny sound like tapping a dinner plate with a spoon, that means sharp shattering ice exploding in my face. The sound I'm listening for is a deep, rich "thunk," a sound like hitting frozen peanut butter with a sledgehammer. When I hear that, I know I can swing, and it will hold my weight. People thought you had to see to climb, but I've found there are many unexpected ways to get to the top of a mountain.

Paul

Practice to Perfect

Signature Systems are not perfected in an instant, or even in the first few attempts. Even if they originate in a flash of brilliance, the final products are the result of tenacity and relentless effort. Most solutions start out as a rough prototype and need some serious polishing. What you think is the answer is usually the beginning of an accelerated road of discovery that may take you somewhere else entirely!

Like the Wright brothers and their first airplane, most possibility pioneers have secret stockrooms packed with failed ideas. Leaders have to recognize this and nurture those strategic trials and early failures within their organizations, if they ever hope to own the kind of Signature Systems that could differentiate their organization in their marketplace. Rough systems you and your team devise will take a lot of work to become smooth, elegant, dependable, and perfect.

As you practice and perfect your new approach, ask yourself:

- How (where, when) can I try out this new system?
- Where (how, when) can I try it again?
- How could I refine this solution?
- Who could give me helpful feedback?
- How much time do I need to get this figured out?

Don't get discouraged! The key to your ultimate success is not brilliance, but sustained effort.

Erik

Paragliding Blind: Possible with Practice

When I decided to try my hand at solo paragliding, I was immediately apprised of all the reasons why this was impossible for a blind guy. But my instructor, Bill, thought differently. He said, "I'm not exactly sure how you'd do it, but I bet there's a way. If you're willing to try, I'll help you."

As we began to train, we found that many parts of paragliding were tactile, not visual. I learned to memorize each of the lines running from my harness to the wing, so I could feel any tangles before a flight. Taking off entailed running like crazy down a steep slope, directly into the wind. Paragliders use thermals, columns of heat rising up from the ground, to get lift. I found that I could feel when I came in contact with a thermal by the way the front of my wing lifted up and tipped me backward.

However, as Bill put it succinctly, "For you, the biggest obstacles will be steering and landing." For steering, Bill would talk me down from the base of the hill via two radios that hung from my neck. There were two just in case the first failed. If they both failed, Bill had a bullhorn.

When you are paragliding, you've got to slow yourself down dramatically as you come in for a landing by pulling the toggles that you hold in front of you. Otherwise you can smack the ground at fifty miles per hour. Bill could tell me when to flare over the radio, but if he got hurt or I had to make an emergency landing, I needed to be able to do it independently.

We discussed solutions such as a talking altimeter, but it wasn't reliable or precise enough. We finally settled on the decidedly low-tech idea of attaching a long string to my harness, with a bell tied onto the end. If everything went right, the bell would ring when it hit the ground and tell me when to flare.

The early landings were pretty rough as we experimented with bells of different sizes and different lengths of string. The first bells were too small; I never heard them. So we attached a giant cowbell that I not only could hear, but also could feel through my body as it thunked the ground. I learned that you descend much faster at higher elevations, so the string needed to be lengthened. You descend slower when the wind is blowing toward you, so the string needed to be shortened. With all these systems working together, even a blind guy manages to execute a perfect stand-up landing every now and then.

My climbing partner, Jeff Evans, looks on during my first solo paraglide, near Boulder, Colorado.

Paul

The Pioneer's Legacy

In every walk of life, pioneers have the most amazing stories. Each story is as unique as the individual behind it, but the stories share a common plot. Pioneers and pioneering organizations have a worthy goal, they struggle to devise some solution to their challenge, and they practice until their Signature Systems are perfect. They fail, rework the system, and then practice more, until the solution works and can be confidently employed. At that point, the impossible has become possible—not just for the pioneer, but for everyone who follows.

What will be the legacy of your breakthrough? What other possible applications does your solution have? Who else will be enriched by what you've done? The next person to benefit from your Signature Systems could be across the globe, or across your kitchen table.

Erik

Parenting Blind: Systems for Success

One of the deepest benefits of pioneering possibilities is how readily it spreads from one area of your life to another. My wife, Ellen, and I have a beautiful daughter, Emma. Before Emma was born, I worried a lot about how I would raise a child when I couldn't catch a ball, play board games, or even change diapers. Actually, with diapers, I tried to convince Ellie that I couldn't do it. Unfortunately, I had just returned from Mount Everest and she wasn't buying it.

My daughter, Emma, and I play our favorite board game together, Candy Land. A friend adapted the game by overlaying each color on the board with a different texture so I can guide my figure on the way to Candy Castle.

To be completely involved in raising Emma, I devised and then practiced some Signature Systems of my own. A friend helped me adapt board games like Candy Land, so that each step on the path to Candy Castle is labeled with distinct tactile squares of material. I found children's books with the words in both type and Braille, so I can read Emma her bedtime stories. I found big inflatable balls that we could play catch with, and that don't hurt so much when she pegs me in the head. I installed a big wrestling mat in our basement so Emma and I can tumble around without getting hurt. Together Ellie and I devised a system for locating Emma when she's nearby. The rule is that whenever I ask, "Where are you?" Emma has to say, "Right here, Dad," right away. Hiding or playing silent is not allowed.

Over the years, we have refined these systems to the point where I now feel reasonably confident as a dad. It turns out I like parenthood so much that Ellen and I decided to inject our lives with an even bigger challenge and blessing. We decided to give Emma a sibling and to adopt a little boy from Nepal, to hopefully give him a good life. When Arjun Lama, age five, finally arrived in the Weihenmayer household, I was ready with some new systems to handle the chaos of two.

Paul

Pioneering Partners

So far this discussion has primarily been about pioneers acting alone—individuals who, like Erik, needed to devise new ways to do familiar tasks, or new ways to take on new challenges. Sometimes these individuals are at the head of an organization, and must lead their company into a new direction for an old purpose, or a new direction for a new purpose. But pioneers also can partner up to face the same challenge together and, in the process, leverage the effectiveness and success of each member of the team for a cause greater than all of them.

My new son, Arjun Lama, and I walk together along a path in Kathmandu, Nepal, during our first visit.

Erik

Towering Possibilities: No Barriers

Wouldn't all of us love a confident voice in our heads telling us which path is credible and which is folly? Unfortunately, that's never the case. All we get is a faint little murmur in our ear, eventually compelling us to act.

A few years ago, I got a phone call from my hero, Mark Wellman. He wanted to climb one of the Fisher Towers, an 800-foot vertical rock pinnacle in Moab, Utah, but there was one catch. He wanted to accomplish this adventure as a party of three disabled climbers, and he invited me to join the team. I knew we'd be the most unlikely team ever assembled, but there was that little voice again, whispering in my ear, telling me this might be possible.

When Mark Wellman was nineteen years old, he fell down a peak in the Sierra Nevada and broke his back. The news that he would never walk again shook the very foundation of his spirit, but that didn't deter him from going through painful rehabilitation; building up his shoulders, back, and arms; and eventually learning to climb again.

Mark invented an ingenious climbing system in which he wore a body harness attached to an ascender, a mechanical device that bit into the rope like teeth, making it possible to slide up the rope but not down. Above this he attached a modified pull-up bar to the rope, also by an ascender. Mark would then slide the bar up the rope as far as his arms would reach. When it locked off, he would hang from it and do a pull-up to its base. Then he would rest a second and repeat the whole process. With the stretchy rope and the wobbly bar, each pull-up gained Mark only about six inches. Five years after his accident, Mark climbed the famous 3,300-foot rock face of El Capitan in Yosemite National Park with this device. It was estimated he did about seven thousand pull-ups in seven days.

Hugh Herr was our second partner. Seventeen years old and already a brilliant rock and ice climber, Hugh summited New Hampshire's Mount

Washington in a February blizzard, got turned around, and descended the wrong side of the mountain. Lost in the forest for three days, he broke through river ice and his legs developed frostbite. Eventually they had to be amputated below the knees. Hugh went on to get a doctorate in engineering at the Massachusetts Institute of Technology, where he developed extremely lightweight prosthetic legs and innovated special detachable climbing feet. He had two kinds, both much smaller than adult human feet, made from the same sticky rubber used in climbing shoes. One pair he attached vertically, wedging them into cracks; the other was a horizontal pair he used to stand on tiny pockets and ledges. Five years after Hugh lost his legs, he had become a better climber than he was before his accident. He was ranked one of the top ten climbers in America. Magazines called him the first "six million dollar man." Hugh jokingly attributed his success to being twenty pounds lighter.

Along the two-mile trail to the base of Fisher Towers, I got the privilege of carrying Mark piggyback style, his legs resting on my curled arms as I strained to jab my trekking poles out in front of us. With all 170 pounds of him on my back, his muscular arms clutching my neck, we resembled a character from an out-of-control video game with a defective joystick. Mark desperately called out directions like "cliff on the left" "boulder on the right," while I jerked and swerved to avoid the dangers.

Hugh led the six rope lengths, his rubber feet delicately balanced on protrusions the width of a dime; I came second, continuously scanning my hands and feet across the rock; and Mark came last, his powerful arms hauling up his lifeless legs in his herky-jerky style. The day was growing colder, and it was beginning to snow. I yelled down to Mark, "You got an extra pair of gloves? It's so freaking cold, Hugh can't even feel his legs." Hugh only grunted.

At the summit, we sat together. The wind blew, and it snowed even more heavily. Mark finally broke the silence, "Not bad for three gimps, huh?"

From that experience, Mark was inspired to start No Barriers, a nonprofit organization designed to teach people with special challenges the most cutting-edge ideas, approaches, and technologies that can help them blast through their own personal barriers to live more adventurous lives. Hugh and I joined the effort, too. The three of us had each struggled to develop new ways to push the envelope, and it was now time to reach out and help others find ways to accomplish their dreams, no matter what it took.

In 2007, we held our third No Barriers Festival, in Squaw Valley, California. Six hundred participants, mostly paraplegics, amputees, blind people, and those with traumatic brain injuries, converged to interact with adventurers, scientists, and researchers who were pioneering new approaches and designing the latest assistive technologies. The demonstration seemed more like science fiction than reality. Hugh Herr, now a world-renowned scientist at MIT, showed revolutionary prosthetic legs with computer-controlled knee and ankle joints that enable above-the-knee amputees to walk—often for the first time. Mark Wellman led mountain bike tours for paraplegics using an innovative hand-crank cycle that allows them to go off-road where wheelchairs can't maneuver. A blind technologist led blind people on hikes solely with the use of a talking Global Positioning System to guide the way.

I got to experiment with an incredible new device called BrainPort. On my head was mounted a small video camera that translated visual information to a half-dollar-size display that in turn presented a tactile image on my tongue. Hundreds of tiny pixels tingled on my tongue, and together they comprised shapes and patterns my brain was able to interpret as a visual picture. I used the BrainPort to read words and numbers on a note card. Since then, I've used it to find holds when rock climbing. I've played tic-tac-toe and rock-paper-scissors with my daughter, Emma. The best part was when Emma stood in front of my head-mounted video camera and I "saw" her smiling face for the very first time.

Whenever we attempt something new and untested, we'll always face some of the most pervasive forms of adversity: doubt and uncertainty. As pioneers, we're always climbing blind. We reach into the darkness, predicting, calculating, hoping, and praying we'll find what we're after, while

Emma and I play tic-tac-toe using the BrainPort technology, which allows blind people to "see" using their tongue rather than their eyes.

understanding there are no guarantees. We commit our minds and bodies to the attempt, knowing it is virtually impossible to reverse course. The fear of failure can be overwhelming—the fear of flopping on our faces, of looking stupid in front of our friends and colleagues, of learning that we aren't as good at something as we thought, or the fear that we've peaked out and can't climb any higher. If we allow it, those fears will paralyze us.

Life is an ongoing reach toward immense possibilities, which are un-seen and only sensed. Yet through that reach, we redefine our limits and capabilities, and shine a light for others to follow.

Pack Light, Pack Right

VINSON MASSIF

Base Camp: 7,000 feet
Summit: 16,066 feet
Vinson Massif is the tallest peak in Antarctica.

It is not length of life, but depth of life.
—RALPH WALDO EMERSON

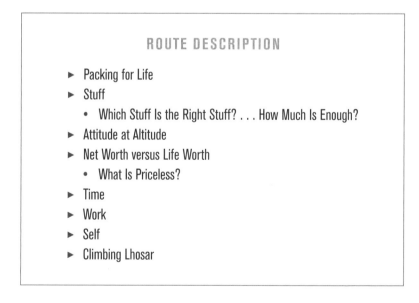

ROUTE DESCRIPTION

- ▶ Packing for Life
- ▶ Stuff
  - • Which Stuff Is the Right Stuff? . . . How Much Is Enough?
- ▶ Attitude at Altitude
- ▶ Net Worth versus Life Worth
  - • What Is Priceless?
- ▶ Time
- ▶ Work
- ▶ Self
- ▶ Climbing Lhosar

Erik

It's pretty tough to climb a mountain if you pack too much, or if you pack incorrectly. Likewise, it's pretty tough to be agile and effective at harnessing adversity each day if you're weighed down by competing priorities vying for your attention. Everyday distractions can bury the potential for everyday greatness. Life is simply too short and too precious to get sidetracked by anything or anyone who depletes our potential to become and to do our best.

Whenever I pack my gear for an expedition, I wrestle with the same questions: What do I need, and what can I do without? There's usually a big difference between what I *want* to bring and what I actually *must* bring. I think the same principles apply to life. You may have something worthwhile you want to do, but you don't know how to pack for your journey. You are encumbered by extra baggage in the form of doubts, preconceived ideas, and tangential obligations. Your map may include a lot of dead ends or long detours. The higher you climb, the more strategic and focused you have to be with your packing and planning.

For Chris Morris and me, just getting to Antarctica was a lesson in packing light and packing right. A single old military cargo plane makes the harrowing six-hour flight across the Drake Passage, attempting it only when the near-constant Antarctic winds die down enough for the plane to land. Since it can carry just enough fuel for the round trip, every ounce of weight counts. Each passenger is allotted a strict hundred-pound baggage limit, which includes personal gear plus a portion of team gear. One hundred pounds seems like it should be plenty, but when you are contemplating a three-week expedition in which you burn five thousand calories a day and temperatures drop to −50°F, the tendency is to overpack.

Since no one checks the body weight of passengers as they step onto the plane, some climbers, looking for a way to cheat the system, have discovered a baggage limit loophole. They stagger on board, dripping with

Chris Morris and I on the summit of Vinson Massif, the highest point on Antarctica. At −50°F, our beards were frozen, and, when I peed it was frozen before it hit the ground.

sweat in the seventy-degree Chilean sun, dressed in their down suits and giant plastic boots, with espresso makers and satellite phones stuffed down their pants. Although I knew the weight limit was a very serious matter, I couldn't help cramming a five-pound bag of peanut M&Ms into my own down suit. Chris Morris had three giant sausages tucked away in his. Everyone was so weighed down that teammates were helping each other in and out of their seats.

Because Chris and I had sat at the tip of South America for nine days waiting out bad weather, we arrived in Antarctica way behind schedule. The pilot who dropped us at Base Camp now told us he'd be back to pick us up in one week—scarcely enough time for us to summit, and leaving absolutely no room for further weather delays. We'd need to move very fast. Typically, Mount Vinson climbers have so much gear that they're forced to make double carries to each subsequent camp: lugging a load to a high camp, then returning to low camp for another load before moving up. Chris and I no longer had this luxury so we'd only have time for single carries. We spent the next two hours reorganizing and paring down provisions so we'd be able to haul everything up the glacier in one push.

For the next several days, Chris and I carried packs and pulled big sleds, but to get to high camp, we'd be navigating through an icefall and up a steep headwall. Eventually the sleds would have to stay behind. We'd be limited to those things we could physically carry on our backs. So at Camp One, I was again faced with the classic mountaineering quandary—what to leave and what to bring. I forced myself to pause and focus, carefully thinking about every piece of gear I might need from head to toe. Certain items were essential for the final push, such as two pairs of thick gloves in case one is blown away. In Antarctica, if fingers become exposed to the elements for even one minute, they can be lost to frostbite.

What could I do without? My toothbrush came to mind. While I had already cut off the handle to save weight, I chose to endure bad breath for a few days and left it behind. Down booties, extra socks, my precious Walkman, and even my peanut M&Ms all went next. I loaded my pack with only the essential gear, hauled it onto my back, quickly realized I could never carry it all, and began again the painful process of deciding what else I could live without. Our med kit, originally the size of a shoe box, was whittled down to fit in a plastic Ziploc bag. An ice axe could double as a splint to traction a broken femur, and duct tape would now patch a bleeding wound as well as a ripped tent.

One dilemma was gnawing at me, however. Before our trip, a television show asked us to carry a video camera to the summit. I reluctantly agreed. I recalled one of my climbing partners who once cut all the tags off his climbing clothes, piled the tags on a scale, and proclaimed proudly, "I just saved four ounces. Now I can bring an extra energy bar!" I had laughed, yet at the same time, I knew that if I were caught in a terrible storm for a week, four ounces of extra food might just be the difference between life and death. In this light, bringing the video camera seemed like sheer lunacy, but I had made a commitment, so it went into my pack.

Two days later, we left early for the summit from high camp as soon as it was warm enough to physically move. In my pack were only the necessities, with the exception of the pesky video camera. At twenty pounds, the pack felt light on my shoulders, but eight hours later it transformed itself into what mountaineers refer to as "the Pig." I was in great shape, but "the Pig" was slowing me down to a crawl. Chris, as usual, yelled for me to hurry up. "Visibility's dropping!" he shouted. "A storm's definitely coming in." After all the training, sacrifice, and waiting, a six-pound video camera was about to cost me the summit. So I yanked the camera from my pack and left it in the snow to be picked up on the way down.

Five hundred feet higher, we were still moving too slow. The wind was now picking up, forcing us to brace against it. Finally, Chris and I made the decision to drop our packs altogether and go for it. I stuffed an energy bar, a little water, and the extra pair of gloves into my down suit. We had climbed higher and gotten closer to our goal, and my perspective on the things I really needed had sharpened and narrowed—just like the mountain itself.

Right below the summit, we faced the greatest test, a narrow rocky

PHOTOGRAPH BY JAMIE BLOOMQUIST

Packing becomes perilous when you have to balance survival against victory. On Vinson Massif, my backpack seemed to get heavier and heavier every step of the way, until it became "the Pig," slowing me down and threatening the success of the climb.

ridge. The frigid wind hammered us as I carefully felt my way across, but I felt secure and strong. I had been freed from the Pig. I thought about all the weighing, considering, and contemplation that had gone into each part of the ascent, and realized it's no coincidence that the word *deliberation* contains within it the word *liberation.*

On the summit, the weather was close to fifty below zero. My legs were cramping and Chris told me my lips were blue from cold. Believe it or not, when I took a leak, the pee actually froze before hitting the ground, and that became my new, personal definition of cold. As far as that video camera I had dumped—well, the television executives would have to settle for footage of Chris eating M&Ms and sausage at Base Camp.

By the next day, the wind and blowing snow near the top of Vinson were ferocious. If we had added just one more day hauling extra gear, we wouldn't have made it. Instead we had stood on the top of Antarctica.

Although climbers flying to Vinson cheat the system by stuffing extras into their down suits, you can't really cheat in life. We either pack with deliberation for what's important to us, or we are crushed by an array of diversions. If we pack light and pack right, we set ourselves free, so that when adversity rises up in the path of what really matters, we are poised to harness its tremendous power.

Paul

Packing for Life

One lesson that is constantly reinforced by my business clients, which applies to each one of us, is this: When we are constantly drained by the sheer weight of our obligations, it's nearly impossible to move toward being great. This chapter is about maintaining your agility, energy, and focus so you can perform your own alchemy. It will equip you with the principles of packing for life, so that all the factors—including your resources, time, work, fuel, and health—are aligned properly for you to ratchet your way up the Adversity Continuum. You will shed unnecessary burdens that may be sapping your strength, or slowing down your organization. Like the other Summits, this one addresses you both as an individual, and as a member of a team, family, organization, and community.

What obligations do you currently carry through life? How much of what you do is really climb-critical? How much of it is really just consuming your resources? Ultimately, do the things you pack into your life—the items you accumulate, the decisions you make, the work you do, the ways you invest your time and money, the way you manage your own health—weigh you down or lift you up?

Proper packing takes clarity and discipline, especially in the face of adversity. At the most basic level, we have too many material items. We have more choices and stuff than at any time in history. Stuff costs money. Stuff adds complexity. Stuff demands mindshare. And money spent on one thing means money not spent on something else.

We also can be burdened by obligations. If your calendar is full, you don't have the freedom to pursue new opportunities that arise suddenly. Without room for spontaneity, you are forever trapped in the same routine. Being scheduled two years in advance does not allow you to turn on a dime when your circumstances change.

And finally, we can be weighed down by our thoughts. What we carry in our minds may be the most important of all. Our attitudes and assumptions can give us wings, or feet of clay.

Stuff

You can never get enough of what you don't need to make you happy.
— ERIC HOFFER

Everyday greatness means rising above mediocrity, even when its gravitational pull is enormous. It means moving forward and up, when everyone else is camping. Sometimes it can even mean escaping comfort and welcoming adversity.

Recreational campers can load a giant RV to the hilt with every comfort of home. Sure, all that stuff will compromise their gas mileage, slow them down on the curves, and take up some space, but they're just trying to get to the next campground to plug in and hang out. You might say that they are on an adversity-free quest—to make the journey as easy as possible. They willingly sacrifice agility for comfort because they aren't looking to get away from it all. To get deep into nature or far from crowds, they would have to travel light.

Do you spend so much energy earning dollars for more stuff that you have sapped your ability to convert adversity into fuel for some higher quest? Have you ever missed one of your kids' events, or a gathering with good friends, because you decided to take on that extra project to help pay off some self-induced bills? Are you so weighed down with all your commitments that it becomes less and less possible to pursue otherwise rich opportunities? Has there ever come a time in your life when "more" has become "less"?

You don't have to be slogging extra weight up a mountain in Antarctica to realize less is sometimes more—and more can be less. According to Gregg Easterbrook, author of *The Progress Paradox*, however you measure it, Americans (we are by no means alone in this) are better off and have gained greater material wealth in the past fifty years than at any other time in our history. His entire book and supporting research is dedicated to the subject of how more stuff leads to no more happiness, and in some cases less happiness.

Our middle class enjoys greater luxuries than the highest royalty of the not-so-distant past. Today's ordinary time-savers and lifestyle enhancers such as washing machines, desktop computers, automobiles, telephones, refrigerators, dishwashers, ovens, microwaves, and—for many people—even running water were all unimaginable a mere century ago. Over recent decades, the average home in the United States has grown from 1,100 to nearly 2,400 square feet and has added more rooms for fewer people. More people own homes, packed with more stuff at higher prices. Nonetheless, more than half of us report that life is getting worse. When it comes to material gains and happiness, more of the first does not necessarily lead to more of the second. In fact, the inverse can be true. More stuff leads to more complexity, which leads to less time, less peace of mind, and a lessened capacity to take on important challenges. Sometimes the more we add, the weaker we become. Then, when adversity hits, the old reflex to "Take It On" becomes a plea to "Take It Away!" The key is acquiring those things that truly enrich us and fuel us, while at the same time developing the discipline to shed those things that do not.

The more stuff we have, the more we have to maintain and manage, and the less nimble we become. So, whatever we stuff into our lives, or our kids' lives, or our homes, bodies, grocery carts, and daily calendars, we all face the basic question . . .

Which Stuff Is the Right Stuff?

Do you have the right stuff—those things that directly help, rather than hinder, your everyday greatness? We're not usually taught to think of our money or our stuff in these terms.

Want versus need. That is the rub. It takes tremendous honesty to separate the two. I'm always asking myself and others,

"What is climb-critical?" What is truly essential to accomplishing the most important things? And what is merely desirable? My humble observation is that, as a society, once we move beyond genuine need to expected desires, we enter the potentially ugly culture of entitlement. Most of us spend much of our resources on things we want, but do not need. Our requirements are food, water, shelter, safety, and arguably love. Everything else falls somewhere on the continuum of desires from "fairly essential" to "completely frivolous."

The right stuff most enables and least hinders your efforts to deliver your own version of everyday greatness—to accomplish the things you are meant to do in life. Muster the discipline to apply this criterion to all your belongings, and only the right stuff remains.

How Much Is Enough?

Since most of us live well beyond "need" and well within "want," most of what we have is, by definition, unnecessary. Tough, but true. However, pleasures are not evil. They need not detract from your higher calling. In fact, they can enhance your well-being and enable you to make your best effort. Climbers need to rest and rejuvenate themselves. They need to have fun in order to be able to focus on the next piece of rock. But once pleasures obscure or, worse yet, become your calling, you have a problem.

Whenever you purchase something, consider tossing something. Ask yourself: Will this help me do what I am meant to do? Take on only those pleasures that truly enhance and never impede your path; those that leave you fueled, agile, and ready to take on your life's adversities.

Erik

Attitude at Altitude

On Mount Everest, the Sherpas are in a league of their own. Their hardiness and toughness are legendary. Some have pulled off superhuman feats of prowess, including climbing from base camp to summit in just over ten hours, as well as spending twenty-four hours in a tent perched on the summit itself.

When Jeff Evans and I were on Everest at about 25,000 feet, heading up to high camp, we passed a Sherpa who was heading down. Jeff and I were wearing $800 one-piece down suits, space-age boots, and oxygen masks pressed over our faces. In contrast, the Sherpa was wearing hand-me-down plastic boots and a pair of jeans several sizes too large. His oxygen mask was hanging ineffectually around his neck, and just to rub it in a little more, he was smoking a Marlboro. Western doctors specializing in high-altitude medicine have performed numerous studies on the Sherpas to determine the cause of their obvious advantages, and their findings repeatedly come out the same: no significant physiological differences can be found.

So if Sherpas aren't simply born with some kind of physical advantage, what is their secret? Personally, I think it comes down to their lifestyle. On their off-season, they eke out an existence growing barley and potatoes in the hard, rocky soil. They live in cold rock huts in high-altitude pastures grazing their yaks. Just to get to the next village, they walk uphill for miles, often schlepping a load so massive it would topple most Westerners. I had trained for Mount Everest for two hard years, punishing my body by putting myself into the most arduous and miserable environments I could find, and that *still* didn't equal the everyday travails of Sherpa life. The rigors experienced on the slopes of Everest are simply a natural extension of their everyday lives.

Similar to the Sherpas, the Eastern Europeans and Russians also have a reputation for being hard climbers. After the Berlin Wall came down in 1988 and the world's great mountains were opened to the Soviet-bloc countries, climbers from Poland, the Czech Republic, Slovenia, and Russia began distinguishing themselves from their Western counterparts. In the next fifteen years, these teams racked up a series of first ascents on the world's tallest peaks, on the most difficult faces, and in the middle of winter.

On Everest one evening, we pitched our tent next to two teams that were heading down the mountain. To our right was an American team that had fallen short of the summit. The three Americans were lounging in a deluxe tent built for five, complete with high ceilings and plenty of room for gear, feasting on "Annie's All-Natural Pasta and Chicken Parmesano."

On the other side of us were eight Russian climbers who had successfully put up an impressive new line on Lhotse Shar, an even more difficult peak than Everest. Their route was steep and radical, and it wasn't too hard to understand why it had remained unclimbed until that point. All of the Russians were crammed into a tent for five, with several holes patched up with duct tape. They had lived for weeks on instant mashed potatoes mixed with a bouillon cube for flavor. Instead of hot drink mixes, their team had used and reused a handful of tea bags. While climbing to the summit, instead of consuming sweet, crunchy energy bars, they survived on an unpleasant substance called Gailtaler speck: pig fat dried and condensed into a hard block. After sharing some conversation, I learned they had spent twelve hours up high hanging from the face in their harnesses. "That must have been terrible," I remarked to one of them. He simply grunted, "Cold! Just like my apartment in Novosibirsk." In the Eastern-bloc countries, three generations of a family might live, sleep, and eat in a one-bedroom apartment, with the heat working only occasionally. So living in a tent on a mountain wasn't viewed as deprivation or sacrifice, but as a grand escape—the ultimate vacation.

Many have marveled at what the Sherpas, Eastern Europeans, and Russians have been able to accomplish despite a lack of material wealth. I believe, however, their admirers have it backward. Their no-frills lifestyles are a kind of gift. The discipline and perspective gained through their ordinary lives have given them the perfect foundation to achieve greatness.

PHOTOGRAPH BY DIDRIK JOHNCK

Despite their secondhand gear and lack of formal training, the Sherpas on Mount Everest are in a league of their own, renowned for their hardiness, toughness, and feats of heroism.

Paul

Net Worth versus Life Worth

The cost of a thing is the amount of . . . life which is required
to be exchanged for it, immediately or in the long run.
—HENRY DAVID THOREAU

You've probably noticed that people who demonstrate any sort of greatness use their money to elevate, not accumulate. They use it to help fund challenges, rather than to distance themselves from facing challenges. Money has strategic importance. It is a way to fund what matters most, not to demonstrate who has the most.

When you add up all your assets (the value of everything you have) and subtract all your debts (everything you owe), you arrive at your net worth. I encourage you to apply this formula to your life. Take into account all the positives in your life (everything that is enriching—both the love, charity, kindness, thoughtfulness and energy you give, and the peace, fulfillment, and contentment you receive), and subtract all the negatives (everything that harms or diminishes your quality of life). What is your Life Worth? Ouch! Tough question!

If you are unhappy with your answer, reconsider how you are handling the adversities in your life. Properly used, adversity feeds Life Worth.

You can stand on a mountain of net worth and be utterly miserable, but you cannot stand on a mountain of Life Worth and be anything less than fulfilled. How happy are you with your balance of net worth and Life Worth? How close is it to where you wanted to be by this age and stage in life? Do you let the pursuit of comfort get in the way of your higher cause—everyday greatness? Or are you using adversity, at the cost of comfort, to grow Life

Worth—perhaps suffering a little, but making focused, purposeful sacrifices today for a long-term greater good? How pleased are you with the way you have handled the challenges you've been given, or those you've chosen?

Given a choice, nine out of ten people would prefer to have more Life Worth than net worth. Some choose the max on both. While a lot of people set off to accumulate net worth at the expense of Life Worth, it is extremely rare that someone ultimately chooses higher net worth than Life Worth as the ideal. Why not choose all Life Worth and no net worth? Because most of us are not willing to live like Mother Teresa, who likely had phenomenal Life Worth, but died with only her robe, sandals, Bible, and rosary beads. Using the next dollar of net worth to directly fund Life Worth—to use the fruits of your hard-fought adversities to grow a richer life—that's what it's all about.

What Is Priceless?

Within the first years of our marriage, Ronda and I faced some unexpected adversity. One day she was standing in the kitchen and a jar of strawberry preserves she was holding just slipped right out of her hands. It was both odd and chilling. We shared a moment of silent, amazed fear. Not one to complain, she finally revealed that she had been wrestling with a strange tingling in her head, and that sometimes her hands didn't work so well. She had been holding off telling me, for fear that it might be a brain tumor, something from which a friend had recently died. She just hoped the problem would go away.

We scheduled a visit to the doctor. I remember the incredible sense of intimacy with her and the vulnerability I felt for her as I watched the MRI scans of her brain. The diagnosis, confirmed by two doctors, was irrefutable. Ronda had multiple sclerosis, or MS. Our doctor explained, matter-of-factly, that MS is progressive. It can be aggressive or episodic, devastating or manageable, fast or slow. There was no way to know which one she had. We just knew that life, as we had known it, was forever changed. How it was changed seemed largely up to us. My paternal grandfather, whom I had never met, had died of MS at an early age. I knew its potential to utterly decimate a person. We were determined to do all we could to reduce the chances that Ronda would ever suffer such a fate.

Months before this watershed event, a prominent venture capitalist had taken a tremendous interest in my AQ-based business, convincing me and my team that, "because of the uniqueness and robustness of your intellectual capital," we could develop one of the largest training and consulting firms in the world. We found the idea of such far-reaching impact exciting. This venture capitalist saw the huge potential profit as the real measure of success. He was fond of saying, "Remember, it's not a crime to be filthy rich!"

My prospective partner made it clear that to create such an enterprise would require nonstop, relentless dedication, for at least the first few years. And it would induce "unprecedented stress." Some of us thought he was being melodramatic, but I sensed that he was more right than wrong, maybe even conservative in his estimate. I was pumped by the challenge, so we began to go down the promising path of building PEAK Learning into a global powerhouse in earnest. We looked at office space, assembled Wall Street investors, and more. The wheels were in motion. Then came Ronda's diagnosis.

So here we were at this critical juncture in our lives. Net worth versus Life Worth. We had two wonderful young boys, Chase and Sean. Ronda had just been diagnosed with MS, and there was no guarantee that she'd be able to walk the next morning, or ever again. Being with my family was the most important aspect of my life—and still is. On the other hand, I had an opportunity, which in all likelihood would never come again, to be CEO of a major company. Perhaps it would go public, and I could retire early with a big vault bulging with money, with which we could do as we pleased. I even began to rationalize that, if I could come out the other side of the tunnel of relentless sacrifice within five years, we would have additional resources to help deal with anything that might go wrong. Even though building the company would require enormous compromise and constant travel, it could prove to be the noblest thing to do. Right?

Choices like these are highly personal, and I know that my choice would not be right for everyone. But the thought of missing whatever good days were left with our family all together—days free from the more serious hardships that could be brought on by MS—was unacceptable. To me, no amount of money was worth selling out my family, our togetherness, and the freedom to be there with and for Ronda, just in case.

Today, the same dynamic tension continues in a different fashion. Ronda's diagnosis made me shift my focus from quantity-of-dollars to quality-of-life. I limit my travel to 25 percent, which means I have to say "no" as frequently as "yes" to client requests. Ronda still has MS. But to this day, decades later, we've been enormously blessed that she has been able to keep it largely at bay by exercising, eating right, strengthening her mind, and living sensibly. In fact, if you were to attend one of her workshops on "You're Only Young Twice," or one of the fitness classes she leads at the health club, you'd never have a clue about the battle she fights every single day.

Although I'd do anything to take Ronda's illness from her and make it mine, I'm immensely grateful for the ways in which it helped us to reorder our lives around what matters most. One of the gifts of adversity is its unique power to press the "reset" button on what we pack into life. For Ronda, the boys, and me, it made us rethink how we invest our time and resources. Ronda now has the most intense appreciation of life—and it's infectious. Whatever your adversity may be, it can become your personal elevator to the top of the Adversity Continuum, where you enjoy a level of Life Worth you could never have achieved without your hardship.

Time

How we spend our days is, of course, how we spend our lives.
—ANNIE DILLARD

Time is a far more precious resource than stuff. Stuff comes and goes. Time just goes.

How do you use your day and spend your life? People who harness adversity have a positive urgency coursing through their veins. Fueled by their latest challenge, they are anxious for the high-octane buzz the next worthy challenge delivers when they Take It On, take it in, and convert it into life-enriching lessons and experiences. Being fully alive is addictive. Just as indifference is the enemy of passion, wasting time is the enemy of achieving everyday greatness, and it is the demon of any enterprise.

Steve Jobs, the legendary CEO of Apple Computer, gave a moving commencement address to Stanford University's 2005 graduating class. In it, he explained how he drives his own Life Worth:

> Your time is limited, so don't waste it living someone else's life. . . . When I was 17, I read a quote that went something like: "If you live each day as if it was your last, someday you'll most certainly be right." It made an impression on me, and since then, for the past 33 years, I have looked in the mirror every morning and asked myself: "If today were the last day of my life, would

I want to do what I am about to do today?" And whenever the answer has been "No" for too many days in a row, I know I need to change something.

How do we balance the need for agility with a calendar full of Life Worth? When we take on too much, we risk becoming "obligation martyrs"—the kind of people who fill their lives with so many responsibilities that they end up burdened with obligations and drained of enthusiasm. When we try to take on every challenge, we run the risk of burning out instead of achieving everyday greatness. It's also easy to get tempted by the things that provide the immediate excitement or rush, over the things that provide long-term benefits.

Your Summit Challenge and Summit Adversity are now your top priorities. As you look at your calendar for the next month, ask yourself which entries are climb-critical. Extraneous demands are only interfering with your ability to succeed where it matters most. Pick two or three things on your calendar that score particularly low on Life Worth, and cross them out.

Work

I believe you are your work.
Don't trade the stuff of your life, time,
for nothing more than dollars.
That's a rotten bargain.
—RITA MAE BROWN

Your job has enormous potential for both Life Worth and adversity. Done wrong, work can be your single biggest burden and drain of energy. Its countless setbacks and annoyances can consume you to the point where you lose your ability to turn the lead of your life into gold. On the other hand, done right, work can be among the most enriching facets of your life.

Your approach to work may mirror and will likely influence the way you live your life outside of work. Most of us mindlessly accumulate the tasks, obligations, and responsibilities that make up our workday with little or no thought to the big picture. But look at it this way: On the job, you have a chance to hone your skills at harnessing adversity, plus you may be able to find opportunities to address your Summit Challenge.

I know some jobs can really stink. But if you attack work, any work, with resolve and creativity, you energize yourself and create positive momentum by turning into the storm. If you approach your job as dead time, or even as just a source of income, you waste a major opportunity to build your Life Worth.

Most jobs won't save the world or transform human life. Most work is more mundane. However, the more mundane your job may be, the greater your opportunity to infuse it with Life Worth. Any job can have meaning if you approach it with a little creativity and the right mind-set. You are the primary source of Life Worth, not external circumstances.

People often feel they are trapped in unfulfilling jobs because they have to pay the bills, or they can't see any way out. Sometimes they feel forced to trade their values and spirits for a paycheck. Your work should enhance, not deplete, your Life Worth. Changing jobs may seem like the obvious way to solve this problem, and you can probably think of someone who left a traditional job to change his or her entire way of life, perhaps to make less money but feel more satisfied. Switching out of your current job is an option, but in many cases it's possible to reinvent how you do what you do to create greater Life Worth. Use the adversities of your workday to some genuine advantage. Infuse whatever work you do with Life Worth so you finish your day energized, or used up in a good way. And that's important, since most of us spend our prime energy hours, and the prime of our lives, on the job.

On the central coast of California, a local fishing pier has two seafood shops that present a marked contrast. It's a working pier jutting about one mile into a large, protected bay in the Pacific Ocean. Sea lions piled three deep bark and loll around on a nearby raft, and seagulls swoop down in hope of the random dropped morsel. Throughout the day small fishing boats unload their modest catches to be cleaned and sold.

On the north side of the pier is a seafood shop with an assortment of the day's catch. It has a price list on a whiteboard outside the window where you shout your order. More often than not, you have to repeat yourself to make sure the person on the other side, who seems viscerally irritated by a customer interruption, acknowledges you with a low grunt before disappearing into the back to package your order. The seafood is fresh, the service a little rough. It's pretty much what you'd expect from such a joint. Good seafood, reasonable price, miserable servers. Can't blame them. Who wants to wrap smelly fish all day in that cold, wet fog?

On the opposite side of the pier, about a hundred yards away, you will find Winston Lee's open-air seafood shop. The first thing you notice is how meticulously clean his tanks, countertops, and deck are—quite a feat for an establishment that is under the relentless onslaught of mildew and raw salt air. Regardless of the weather, crowds, or time of day, Winston greets each customer with a big, warm smile, and often a song.

"I just love what I do," Winston explains. "Good seafood makes everyone happy and healthy. It is the best thing to eat and it helps you live a long life. I have the best job in the world. All day, even in the rain, I make people happy with my seafood . . . because I sell the best seafood anywhere!"

On the surface, Wilson provides the same service as his competitor. But instead of slapping some fish into butcher paper and sending people on their way, Winston honestly cares about enriching people's lives . . . through seafood. He works hard to provide each customer with something extra by offering his advice on recipes, preparations, combinations, and bargains. His pride, resilience, and sense of mission are contagious, and apparently very good for business. People line up at Winston's humble shack, even though the other seafood shop often has greater variety.

Both jobs have plenty of adversity. Fog, cold, rude customers, smelly fish, inconsistent quality, undependable fishermen, and thin profit margins can all add up to a pretty tough day. One shop owner is consumed by adversity. The other consumes it to fuel his day. If Wilson can turn standing out in the open on a cold, wind-battered pier all day long selling seafood into a quest, you can pack almost any job, including yours, with more Life Worth. And when you do, everyone wins.

Self

Look to your health; and if you have it, praise God,
and value it next to a good conscience; for health is the second blessing
that we mortals are capable of—a blessing that money cannot buy.
— IZAAK WALTON

Harnessing adversity takes physical, spiritual, and emotional strength. How far can you ascend if you are physically exhausted and out of shape, spiritually empty, and emotionally spent? Even if you pack your life light and right, with the stuff, obligations, and work that enhance Life Worth, it is still you who must take on the terrain. Agility, alchemy, and adversity demand your best. You have to treat yourself like a world-class athlete so you can give your best to everyone else.

Do a scan of the people you most respect. Chances are most of them invest in themselves as the engine of Life Worth for others. Stephen Covey tells us to "sharpen the saw," or invest time in ourselves before our effectiveness slides. If you are not careful, you can become a martyr by helping others to the point of hurting yourself. The implicit Law of Life Worth says that you can't pour out any more or any better than you take in. That's why active, positive, productive people do not hesitate to schedule time to refuel and rejuvenate. Alchemists focus on the kind of learning, exercise, meditation, relationships, nutrition, and prayer that rejuvenates them—not just for themselves, but first and foremost, for others. They intuitively understand that they have to constantly elevate their own game in order to elevate those around them.

Harnessing adversity is not comfortable. Sometimes you have to take on the unpleasant. As Erik's Eastern European counterparts on Mount Everest demonstrated, you can't pursue only comfort and expect greatness. Erik doesn't train for mountains by walking on a treadmill in a climate-controlled gym while watching television. He trains by running, biking, and climbing along trails and rocks, often in tough conditions so he can maintain his edge. William James said, "Do every day or two something for no other reason than that you would rather not do it." We all have to train for the life we want to live.

Erik has climbed the Seven Summits—the highest peak on each of the seven continents. He has already shattered people's perceptions of what's possible into a million pieces. You might argue that his job is done, his life-goal achieved. And if he retired, like a professional athlete whose contract is up, who would fault him? Climbing is tough business. Yet, for Erik, climbing is but one way to teach others around the world that they can be and do more.

Instead of retiring, Erik begins many days when he's home with a two-hour bike ride up Lookout Mountain with a neighbor who meets him at 5:30 AM at his front door, or by making an intense morning climb with a friend—often a teammate from the Everest expedition—up one of Colorado's "fourteeners" or a nearby rock face. This keeps his body and mind ready for the next big challenge. It also hones him so he can tackle the rest of his workday, writing or preparing for his next talk or meeting. And even though he is one of the top speakers on the corporate circuit, Erik always asks questions—the hallmark of a lifelong learner. He is constantly expanding his mind, much as he expands his soul through the humbling and uplifting nature of his craft.

Why is Erik so relentless in his evolution? Because giving less than his all to his wife, Ellie, and his children, Emma and Arjun, as well as to his friends and clients, is simply unimaginable to him. And by living his example through deeds rather than words, Erik inspires us all to become better, to become more.

I, too, wake up each day striving to live what I teach. Some days I fail. But, if I am going to coach CEOs on how to use these principles to optimize their businesses and their lives, I must do all I can to model these lessons, as a business owner, researcher, husband, father, son, community member, and more. So, at home, I begin almost every day paddle surfing in the ocean. I join my son or a good friend, we throw our kayak-surfboard hybrids (my sons still surf "old-school") into the ocean at the crack of dawn, and we bash through the waves, riding as many as possible for a nonstop hour of aerobic crank, breathtaking natural beauty, and adrenaline-induced fun. With our paddles, we get ten times the number of rides of standard surfers. We see the sunrise, the fog move, and the otters and seals laugh at our antics. It's complete spiritual, emotional, and physical rejuvenation.

Other mornings I run the trails with my dog. I try to really experience the sounds, smells, and beauty of the day. When I'm on the road, I make sure I hit the workout room before each program, no matter how little sleep I've had. It always pays off. On mornings when I'm weary from long or late travel, I am positively haunted by all the people I have the privilege of affecting through my work, in any form, and I drag my bones out of bed and work the energy flywheel by exercising—ideally outside, to get some spiritual benefit as well.

If I am going to be any kind of researcher, I have to feed my mind. I bring a stack of articles and magazines on every airplane flight, and I absorb as much as possible, trying to refresh my thinking. Between flights I am in the newsstand, picking the next books or magazines. In my hotel room, I keep the TV off, and I read or research online. I try to resist easy temptations to feed my body, mind, and soul empty "calories," and to focus on enriching, nutritious fuel. Small investments yield dramatic results.

Most people find it easy to agree wholeheartedly with the concept of Life Worth. They understand that exercise, spiritual fulfillment, and mental challenges make us stronger. They say, "I really should do more exercise (reading, praying, painting, yoga). Wouldn't it be nice if I had the time (money, energy, babysitter) to do that? Wouldn't it be nice if my husband (wife, boss, kids, colleagues, team) let me do those kinds of things?"

I encourage you to ask a different question: "Won't it be great?" Won't it be great when you begin to apply these principles and practices to your own life? Won't it be great to help your organizations and teams rethink what they bring along whenever they take on anything tough or worthwhile? Won't it be great to feel yourself become more focused and effective?

Erik

Climbing Lhosar

The success of every ascent I attempt is largely determined by how effectively my team and I pack and prepare. Slowly, and learning from many mistakes, I have developed the capacity to make the tough choices needed. Nowhere are those choices more important than on a vertical wall of rock or ice, and as I've gained more climbing experience, this is where I'm increasingly putting my efforts. These big, technical faces are exciting and challenging. To have a chance for success, everything has to go perfectly: ultimate efficiency between team members, stable weather, and every ounce of gear serving a critical purpose. On Vinson, we carried our houses on our backs, but it's a step up to carry your house while climbing vertically.

The second reason these faces appeal to me more now has little to do with climbing. Now that I have a family, it feels wrong to be away for the months it takes to climb major high-altitude peaks. By climbing steep technical routes, I can be home in just a couple of weeks. It's a nice balance between the pursuit I love a lot, and the people I love the most.

Until about thirty years ago, climbers lacked the equipment and techniques to make quick and safe ascents of these faces. So they resigned themselves to a style called "siege climbing," in which they inched their way up the face, anchoring permanent ropes to the wall, foot by foot, pitch by pitch, until they reached the top. By the end, they'd have ropes running from top to bottom. This allowed them to summit while never losing their toehold to the ground. The problem was that these attempts would take months of effort, massive resources, and huge, unwieldy teams.

But a few pioneers, equipped with some new tools and a new mindset, and tired of the constraints of siege tactics, saw a different way forward. They called it "alpine-style climbing." In this model, climbers wait for a stretch of good weather and, with everything they need on their backs, commit to an all-out push to the summit. In just a few days, a small team of climbers can accomplish what previously took a month and a small army.

More recently, alpine-style climbing has been taken to the extreme. One by one, radically steep unclimbed faces, previously written off as impossible because of rapidly changing conditions and dangerous rock and icefall, are being knocked off in a fast and light style, defying conventional wisdom and expanding expectations about what is achievable.

In 2001, while heading up the trail to climb Mount Everest, we passed Lhosar, a rivulet of blue ice snaking up a deep cleft surrounded by a vertical jungle of rhododendrons and bamboo. Lhosar is an almost 3,000-foot vertical frozen waterfall in the Himalayas named after the Tibetan New Year. One of Lhosar's most storied early ascents was made by an obsessed Polish climber named Voytek Kurtyka, whose acquaintance with the climb was long and anguished. His first try, in 1994, was barely even an attempt. He only got as far as looking across the valley at the ice mammoth, absurdly steep and covered in mist, before he completely lost his nerve and abandoned the effort for the beaches of India. He found the following years depressing as he contemplated his unfinished business.

His life became a series of pilgrimages. On his second effort to climb Lhosar, he failed to get across the tumultuous river that splits the deep valley at the climb's base. "The water burned like an open wound," he said. It wasn't until his third try that he finally got onto the ice face, with his partner, Maciej Rysula. Only one hundred feet up, they almost lost their will. Flowing water ran down the ice and soaked them to the skin; their ice screws provided no protection in the rotten ice; and an ice block the size of a basketball fell and slammed into Voytek's shoulder, making him sore and stiff. Instead of retreating, they redoubled their efforts and pressed on. By the late afternoon, the steep climbing laid back a little, for a few hundred feet, but, said Voytek, "The hope that we would escape before nightfall came and went like the clouds sailing above the chimney. . . . I held on to my axe like a drunk to a lamppost. Eventually I got down on all fours and crawled toward the end of this troubled day."

It wound up taking them four days to climb and descend after a torturous effort through cold and mist. They began hallucinating from dehydration and exhaustion. On the treacherous down-climb, they got lost in the fog and Maciej took a fall, landing on a ledge and breaking his ankle.

I never forgot the image of Lhosar as it was described by my teammates, and in 2006 I made my first attempt on the climb with my partner, Rob Raker. The climbing conditions were terrible. Temperatures were too warm that winter, dropping only to twenty-nine degrees even in the coldest early morning. In addition, the ice had formed erratically, with car-size daggers pointing down the icy throat of the falls. When the afternoon sun warmed the ice, those daggers could easily cut loose and there would be nowhere to hide.

Despite these conditions, we started up the climb at 3 AM. Rob and I had spent many restless hours analyzing and debating whether we could make it to the top in one day, and whether to bring the extra gear needed to spend the night on a ledge. The weight of sleeping bags, stoves, and fuel would slow us down, but the extra supplies could make the difference between failure and an epic climb. With the warm weather, we decided our safest option was to leave sleeping gear behind, hoping we could climb quickly and get above the dangerous sections before the heat of the afternoon.

With just the two of us, we still had to divide up an exorbitant amount of weight: an extra rope and ice tool, four quarts of water and a pile of snacks, emergency bivouac sacks, and metal ice screws and rock gear used to protect a fall. My pack weighed twenty-five pounds, and only two rope lengths up, we already knew we were moving too slowly. As we stopped to debate what to do, a few large chunks of ice whizzed by our heads and helped us make the call to abandon the effort.

On our second attempt, we fared a little better than Voytek and Maciej. This time Rob and I made the decision to add a third climber to our team, Ian Osteyee. Ian would be crucial in case we had to self-rescue. We also thought a third could speed me up and help me save energy; one partner would bring up the rope, and the other would climb beside me, shouting directions and helping me to stay in the path of least resistance.

We decided to go two weeks earlier in the climbing season, when the temperatures were likely to be colder—but on our arrival, Ian, looking a mile across the valley with binoculars, saw that the ice hadn't fully formed yet. It looked bone-thin, separated by long stretches of bare rock. The worst part was that the top 500 feet, consisting of three colossal overhanging ice mushrooms, appeared insurmountable. There was only one way to find out.

Even moving more quickly as a party of three, we still anguished over whether we could make it to the top in a day. Ultimately we settled on the more conservative approach, and packed light sleeping bags, a stove, and fuel. In order to compensate for the extra weight, we had to pare down our packs, dropping some rock protection and ice screws. As we packed, we knew that these decisions would make or break our chance for success.

By 5 PM, after fourteen hours of climbing and with the steepest part yet to go, we pulled off onto an uncomfortable sloping ledge where I wedged myself between a fixed boulder and the cliff face and huddled shivering in my paper-thin bag. A constant frigid wind gusted down the mountain. I was confident I wouldn't die of exposure, but also knew I wouldn't be sleeping much in the next twelve hours. During the night, lapsing into an uncomfortable half sleep, I kept dreaming I had nodded off on the floor of my living room and, for some reason, the front door had been left wide open. A terrible winter storm blew cold wind and spindrift snow on top of me. Emma, my daughter, shook me awake. "Go to bed, silly Daddy. Why are you sleeping on the floor?" Each time, I'd pop awake, only to realize the miserable predicament I was in.

Ironically, Voytek had bivied on this very spot. Looking up the face at the last pitches, he remarked later, "what I saw scared me. Somewhere high above me, terrible frightening ice glittered in the moonlight. The ice sickle was a monster. This had to be an illusion."

The next morning, we forced our frozen bodies out onto the ice. On the last overhanging pitches, with my body hanging from two sharp tools stuck in the ice, I felt as if my arms were being ripped from their sockets. Then, the metal front points of my crampons skittered out from under me; one of my tools popped out of the crumbling ice, and I found myself hanging by *one* arm, my legs dangling 3,000 feet over the Himalayas. By furiously hammering my tool back into the ice and kicking like crazy, I finally got reattached, and after another hour of desperate climbing, the steepness finally let up, and I rounded the top.

Rob and Ian were there to greet me with encouraging voices and enthusiastic slaps on the back. For the first time in two days, I felt the warmth

After two grueling days and a cold night on a ledge, I topped out on Lhosar, a 3,000-foot vertical ice climb in Khumbu, Nepal. If you look closely, you can see the plumes blowing over the
top of Mount Everest in the background center. Ama Dablam is in the right corner and the village of Namche Bazaar is just left of my helmet.

of the sun touch my face. We still had ten hours of rappelling ahead to get back to solid ground, but I exhaled a long breath, allowing all the exhaustion and uncertainties to dissipate into the cold, thin air, replaced by joy. We had climbed Lhosar!

Alpine climbing isn't the easiest path. It takes countless hours of preparation and a lot of commitment, but I believe it is also more true, more pure, and ultimately more rewarding when the summit is finally achieved. So the main question of this chapter is this: Are you willing to go alpine-style through life, to pack with care and give up the stuff that weighs you down so you can have the greatest impact on your life and the people in it? When you make difficult choices, deciding on a direction and eliminating the extraneous, there will always be sacrifice. If you believe strongly enough in your climb, however, it is possible to embrace the hardships and to be strengthened by them. That's what Summit Six, Suffer Well, is all about.

Suffer Well

MOUNT KOSCIUSZKO

Summit: 7,310 feet
Mount Kosciuszko is the tallest peak in Australia.

I cannot imagine a fate more awful—a fate worse than death—
than a life lived in perfect harmony and balance.

—CARL JUNG

ROUTE DESCRIPTION

- ► What Is Suffering Well?
- ► Good Suffering as a Strategy
- ► What Is the Nature of Your Suffering?
  - • Physical . . . Emotional . . . Mental . . . Spiritual
- ► Do a "Suffer Check"
- ► What Is the Extent of Your Suffering?
  - • How Important Is This Adversity? . . . What Is the Cost? . . . How Severe Is Your Suffering? . . . How Long Must You Suffer?
- ► To Suffer Loss with Love
- ► How to Suffer Poorly
  - • Going Nowhere: Whining and Complaining

- Trying to Hide: Escaping and Blaming
- Identifying: Letting Your Suffering Define Who You Are
- Rationalizing Away the Need to Change
- Painting a Pretty Picture: Pretending and Whitewashing
- Suffering? What Suffering? Anesthetizing and Denying
▶ How to Suffer Well
▶ Carstensz

Erik

Suffering has been a major concern of philosophers and religions through-out time. Confucius, Kant, Nietzsche, and Sartre all recognized pain and suffering as essential strands in the human condition. The Bible, the Torah, the Koran are all filled with stories and lessons about suffering as a means to greater awareness and spirituality. Buddhists use fasting, or denying the body its natural needs, as a pathway to greater purity, peace, and enlight-enment.

Suffering also stands as one of the main themes of the Great Books. When I was a teacher, we discussed classics like Virgil's *Aeneid* and Homer's *Iliad*. They are filled with stories of heroic people who must endure unspeakable pain, loss, and disillusionment in order to lead, rise above di-saster, and emerge victorious. Which of these books still would be "great" if they were stripped of the cathartic theme of human suffering as a means to the development of clarity, character, and faith? Without an exploration of suffering, what would we know about the human spirit and its capacity to endure and ultimately grow?

In Homer's second epic poem, the *Odyssey,* Odysseus has fought a ten-year war to take the city of Troy. Victorious and rich with plunder, he and his crew set sail for Ithaca, his home, surely believing their suffering is now behind them. Instead, the voyage takes another grueling ten years.

The men must confront Cyclops, cannibals, witches, and multiheaded monsters, all of which do their utmost to annihilate them. Eventually, Aeolus, the master of the winds, gives Odysseus a leather bag containing all the winds, which carries them within sight of Ithaca. Curious, the foolish sailors open the bag while Odysseus sleeps, unleashing a massive storm. The ships are hurled backward, losing all their hard-won progress.

Kosciuszko, the tallest peak in Australia, was more of a bump than a mountain at 7,200 feet—by far the easiest of the Seven. The real work of Mount Everest, as well as five other summits, was behind us. We figured Kosciuszko was only a ceremonial finish line. When I told a local Aussie of our plans, he responded, "Ah! What a lovely stroll. I did it with my dog last summer." We planned interviews over a satellite feed to news programs around the world for the moment I finished. We even had a bottle of champagne along with us for a celebratory toast at the top.

However, it seems that whenever we finally let up and assume something will be easy, we are presented with a dramatic reminder that life equals suffering. Climbing my seventh summit felt like a mini-version of the *Odyssey,* as if the winds had been unleashed against us. From the moment we arrived at Kosciuszko, during the Australian spring, a series of huge low-pressure systems, half the size of the continent, repeatedly dumped snow over the mountain. The winds near the top roared at eighty miles per hour. After waiting five days for the weather to clear, and with no improvement in sight, we made the decision to go for it. What match would little Kosciuszko be against hardened mountaineers who had summited the tallest mountains in the world?

Only a half hour out of the parking lot, as the howling wind roared down the slopes and drove hard bullets of ice directly into our faces, I already was questioning the wisdom of continuing. One of my teammates was actually lifted up by the wind and sent sliding a hundred yards down the snow slope. When he waved up that he was fine, and we knew he wasn't hurt, we all let out a relieved laugh.

It seemed like the winds had focused their attention on our team, because next I was struck by a tremendous gust. The wind flung me back

Opening a bottle of celebratory champagne in a howling gale at the summit of Kosciuszko. The liquid sprayed all over my face and Gore-Tex jacket and instantly froze.

into Eric Alexander, who was right behind me, and we both went down in a pile. We were a tangled heap of arms and legs as we slid twenty feet down the hard-packed slope before Eric managed to dig in his ice axe and stop us. Back on our feet and working our way upward again, we were learning a new definition of suffering, and had the bruises and windburn to show for it.

As we got above the tree line, we were faced with an indistinct, wind-scoured landscape, made even more disorienting by the blizzard. Jeff Evans took the lead and had to navigate with a compass. For three hours, we wandered around through the whiteout looking for the actual summit.

Finally, after trudging up a last snow face, with the wind fighting us at every step, Jeff described to me the truck-sized boulder layered in ice that signified my seventh summit. It took four of us holding tightly to our banner to pull it out of my pack and hoist it for a few summit shots as the wind tried to rip it away. Then, sticking stubbornly to our summit celebration, we popped open the bottle of champagne. The cork sailed away, zinging, I assume, past all seven continents on its way down. As I took a drink, the fierce wind tipped the neck of the bottle, caught the liquid, and plastered half the contents across my face and Gore-Tex suit. The irony wasn't lost on us. This summit, typically host to T-shirt-clad tourists, young children, and dogs, was doing its best to blow us off the mountain. In fact, of my Seven Summits, little Kosciuszko's brutal winds topped them all. Nothing else was even close.

If I had confronted that kind of adversity on my first summit, it might have sapped my will to even attempt the others. But along the journey, my tolerance for suffering had expanded, and by the time we reached Kosciuszko's summit, all we could do was laugh. In fact, we must have all looked like lunatics, covered in frozen champagne and braced together against the hurricane-force gale as we howled with laughter. Lovely Kosciuszko had done everything in its power to make our experience as memorable as our ascents of far bigger mountains. Instead of a ceremonial stroll to the finish line, we had to work for every inch—and our accomplishment made us proud.

On the way up Kosciuszko, the wind had been an impediment, driving us back, but as I clipped into skis and headed down, I realized that instead of working against us, the wind might actually work for us. The gale now blew at our backs, and like adversity itself, we used its energy to carry us home. It was a wild ride.

Suffering fulfills two vital purposes. It gives our lives perspective, immunizing us against the countless, more mundane adversities that otherwise would seem so terrible. It also can give our lives depth. Without suffering, our achievements would feel more like bumps than mountains.

Paul

What Is Suffering Well?

Character cannot be developed in ease and quiet.
Only through experience of trial and suffering can the soul be
strengthened, vision cleared, ambition inspired, and success achieved.

—HELEN KELLER

Suffering well means doing so in a way that elevates yourself and those around you. It is the one opportunity for everyday greatness we are all granted.

In business, suffering well means putting up with political backbiting, naysayers, long hours, rejection, uncertainty, constraints on resources, downturns, and drudgery in the name of some higher cause or some worthy breakthrough. It means doing whatever it takes to make things right, when it would be so much easier to simply watch them go wrong. It means getting pierced in the back by a quiver of arrows, taking on sacred cows, putting up with unbearable assignments, embracing impossible deadlines, enduring mindless meetings, suffocating amid incompetence, but sticking to a vision no one else yet embraces. It means paying a price others may be unwilling to pay to achieve a goal others may be unable to reach. It means facing up to the hardships inherent in anything significant, and taking on the task together, not with the hollow words "Good luck, team," but rather with the meatier blessing, "Suffer Well!" Live these words and greatness will emerge.

In business, the finest executives I know share the common capacity to suffer well. They shoulder enormous stress, great uncertainty, weighty responsibility, substantial risk; chronic pressure, and nearly impossible, often competing, demands with the same cheer and determination with which a child chases a puppy. When a leader does not suffer well, the entire organization suffers.

Suffering well means taking in the rich nutrients of life's bitter defeats, emerging more powerful, formidable, and focused as a result. Or, if you are on the downslide, suffering well means using the hardships of your reduced capacity as an impetus to shift your focus from yourself to others. It means feasting off fear and failure, leaving them behind as desiccated remains of battles hard fought and well won. Suffering well means employing positive pessimism to weather even the most dismal days, and to lead others through dark times.

To suffer well is to use hardship to transcend ego, so that you get out of your own way in doing what needs to be done with your life. It means coming to grips with lost opportunities in which you could have suffered better, and thinking about impending opportunities to suffer differently next time. To suffer well is to marinate in the pain, rather than anesthetize yourself against it. It is forging your character and hardening your resolve in suffering's white-hot flame, rather than shielding yourself from its searing heat.

To suffer well is to be the alchemist who converts pain and hardship into momentum and life force. It is to distill and ultimately share the meaning you derive from each difficulty. Suffering well means using your pain to help others, and committing yourself to enriching those closest to you with the pure ore of your deepest strengths when it matters most. Use your adversity to become a better person, demonstrating your highest character and virtue in the face of pain. Suffering well is one of the most noble and important things we can do in life.

After visiting the United States, Mother Teresa said that "the poorest place in the world is not Calcutta, it is here, since although you have everything, you have nothing." Mother Teresa might have been warning us against the pursuit of net worth at the expense of Life Worth. Suffering well can make us richer. Failure to suffer well can leave us impoverished.

It is not enough to simply grasp the concept of suffering well—to say, "Okay, I get it. When life gets brutal I've got to shine with optimism and strength." Words disappear readily in harsh winds, and paint-job optimism cracks under the pressure of pain. We need weather-tested tools we can use when hardship hits. This chapter will show you how to use and transcend your adversity by attacking life with renewed determination.

During the past twenty years and more, when I have been out in the world researching, teaching, and conversing about the human relationship with adversity, I have heard ordinary and extraordinary tales of human suffering. Some are tragic. Many, like Erik's, are deeply inspiring. Over time, I discovered some common themes and lessons that I will share. If this chapter gets you to rethink the role of suffering in work and life, then Erik and I will have accomplished what we set out to do.

Erik

Good Suffering as a Strategy

After standing atop Kosciuszko, I was faced with the question "What's next?" I didn't want to be the "blind guy who once climbed the Seven Summits." I had no desire to be a Camper, resting on past accomplishments. My climbing partner, Jeff Evans, and I thought the idea of climbing, caving, mountain biking, running, rafting, and kayaking against the world's elite adventure racers sounded like an exciting challenge.

Climbing a mountain is tough, but few things have made me suffer more than the 2003 Primal Quest, the toughest adventure race in North America, if not the world. It involved 460 miles, 60,000 feet of elevation gain, nine days, and no time-outs. It started with eighty elite teams from around the world, each composed of four extraordinary athletes, all of whom had to cross the finish line together. If one member dropped, then the team was disqualified.

For practice, our team of four tried a five-day race across Greenland, but because it was only half the distance as the Primal Quest, the pace was twice as fast. With all the teams operating at sprint pace, my team fell days behind. I tore my calf muscle trying to keep up on the rugged terrain, and we ultimately had to drop out.

But we learned. We learned that to have a chance to complete the extreme distance of the Primal Quest, teams would have to gear down and settle into a steady pace. I knew we couldn't beat the other teams on the basis of speed or even skill, but we might just be able to outsuffer them. Suffering actually became the key component of our race strategy.

Shortly after we began the race, it didn't seem like such a bright idea after all. Fatigue began to ravage our bodies, the climbs became increasingly formidable, and as more and more teams dropped out of the race, Jeff and I began to call the race the "Suffer Quest."

The first leg of the race was a thirty-mile, nine-hour kayak across Lake Tahoe. I was in front setting the pace, and it worked well for the first five hours. In the final four, a strong headwind kicked in and caused the cold waves to crash over my head. When we pulled the kayak out of the water, I was hypothermic. But thankfully the next leg, a hundred mile tandem bike ride over the Sierra Nevada, warmed me right up again.

I was still plagued by my calf injury from Greenland. Two days into the race, my injured calf screamed with every step. I thought that if it got any worse, there was no way I would be able to keep moving. Ten hours later, however, my calf was the least of my worries, because my knees felt like they both had been hit with a sledgehammer. Ten hours after that, I couldn't feel the pain in my knees anymore; it had moved to the giant blisters on my toes.

By day four, teams began to drop around us. Some had begun the race too quickly and burned themselves out, others had capsized in the whitewater and had banged themselves up, some participants had gotten heat stroke, and others had gone into shock as their bodies became depleted of electrolytes. One guy, part of a Special Forces team, had fallen asleep riding his bike and crashed. We rode by the paramedics who were cleaning his wounds before transporting him to the emergency room.

Since we were only catching an hour of sleep a night, my team was suffering from sleep deprivation—or, as adventure racers like to say, we had been "bitten by the sleep monsters." At one point, as we were bouncing down a mountain trail at midnight with Jeff guiding us from the front of the tandem, he admitted he couldn't see the trail anymore. His eyes were so fatigued they simply weren't working. As we rode for the next hour, I continually slapped him on the back, sang songs, and told dumb jokes. "Whatever you do, absolutely do not fall asleep!" I yelled in his ear. Finally, he rebounded, but a few minutes later, I fell asleep myself. The bike swerved and I sprang awake.

It seemed that every time we conquered a huge series of hills on the tandem and convinced ourselves we were about to top out, we'd round a corner and be confronted by an even bigger mountain. We couldn't figure out how they had rigged this race with hills that eternally went up and never went down. Rather than being demoralized, though, our response each time was to turn to each other and crack up laughing. I figured it was better than crying.

Stumbling through a forty-mile boulder field on the last night, I was actually hearing hallucinations. Since I was once a teacher, I'd hear my fifth-graders cheering me on from an imaginary playground. I could hear them shaking the chain-link fence and yelling, "Keep going, Mr. Weihenmayer.

Jeff Evans and I descend a downhill section of the Arctic Team Challenge, Greenland, on my tandem mountain bike. We failed to cross the finish line on this first adventure race, but we fared better on our second, the Primal Quest, known as the toughest endurance race on earth. Out of the eighty elite teams that started the race, we were one of only forty-two to cross the finish line nine days later. Our strategy was to outsuffer the other teams.

You can do it!" Jeff was so exhausted, he was also hallucinating, but he had visions of tiny trolls and goblins jumping out of the woods and biting his toes. Of course, Jeff's visions might have had something to do with the hundred Grateful Dead shows he had attended over the years.

Eight days and twenty-three hours after beginning, our team crossed the finish line. We didn't win, but we were one of only forty-two teams to complete the race. No blind person had ever attempted an expedition-length adventure race, and the rumor, I later learned, was that some teams thought we wouldn't make it past the first day.

At the finish line at 4 AM, I heard a giggly little voice yell, "Daddy!" At first I thought I was hallucinating again, but as the voice ran and wrapped its arms around my legs, I realized that Emma and Ellie were there to meet us. That voice made all the suffering of the last nine days worthwhile.

I'm convinced that our ability to outlast and outperform dozens of far more experienced teams was not just due to our fitness, our systems, or our cohesiveness. It also was due to our capacity to outsuffer them.

Suffering seems to be the one experience we all share and the one thing most of us would gladly give up. But suffering can be elevating and transforming, and can also give us just the edge we need when we're trying to do something important.

Paul

What Is the Nature of Your Suffering?

To suffer is to *endure something painful*. Like joy, suffering comes in all shapes, sizes, and durations. The loss of a job or a loved one can be instant and severe. A car accident or stock market crash is highly defined, with potentially enduring effects. Adversities such as ill health, fading friendships, a dying marriage, or boring work may be gradual, amorphous, and vague.

Suffering also is voluntary or involuntary—a distinction that is not always easily determined. Every time people run a marathon, take on a monumental task, or induce a major change, they are *choosing* to suffer. You can see the exhausted exaltation on the face of a sleepless scientist who worked relentlessly to unravel a riveting mystery, or the gratification in the expressions of your team members who suffered real hardships to deliver a superior result. No one forced Erik to climb the Seven Summits. There's something energizing about the hardships that come from stretching your capacity. Voluntarily testing your limits can bring unique pleasure. Self-induced suffering can prove a useful training ground for involuntary suffering, and vice versa. I believe consciously suffering for the sake of bettering or helping something or someone you care about is one of the most elevating things we can do.

Suffering can be categorized in four main areas. Because we are deeply interconnected, suffering in one area is likely to induce suffering in another. It would be easy to treat each type of suffering as if it occured in isolation, but the reality is that most people who suffer in one of the following four ways—physically, emotionally, mentally, or spiritually—suffer to some extent in at least one other way. For example, if you're in physical pain, you are likely to be emotionally upset. Likewise, if you have a problem of vital importance that remains unsolvable (mental suffering), you may begin to feel your God has abandoned you (spiritual suffering).

Physical Suffering

Our bodies tell us when something hurts. If it hurts severely enough and for long enough, we suffer. Physical suffering can occur in an enormous range of experiences, from mild but chronic discomfort like a headache, to being stuck on the airport tarmac for several hours in 112-degree heat with 320 other passengers sharing the same miserably oversold flight, to the most unspeakable physical agonies, which need not be enumerated here.

Emotional Suffering

Worry, fear, frustration, anger, helplessness, resentment, anxiety, envy, anguish, hatred, disgust, and even love are the classic forms of human suffering upon which the poet and playwright draw. Emotional suffering also can hurt physically. It can make your heart ache, your limbs heavy, and your gut twist in knots. Our discovery is that despite their masterful "game face" reflecting cheer and control, most people go through moments, if not extended periods, of significant emotional suffering over the course of a normal week or month.

Unlike physical suffering, emotional suffering can be contagious. One person's worries can easily become another's. This transference can go deep, affecting the chemistry and physiology of other people, as if the emotional suffering originated with them. This is one of the reasons learning to suffer well is so vital—because it reduces the burden we transfer to others.

Our society has created a multibillion-dollar industry solely dedicated to the alleviation and mitigation of physical and emotional pain: pharmaceuticals. Today it is expected that a person suffering physically, and often emotionally, will seek some sort of treatment or solution. Nonetheless, and despite our best scientific advances, our society is full of people who suffer from chronic pain, and as a result suffer more than just physically. This is one reason why other kinds of suffering are likely to kick in over time.

Mental Suffering

When we can't seem to figure out and resolve a matter of great importance, we suffer mental anxiety. We may agitate over how to care for an aging parent; how to graduate before our student loans run out; how to fit in time with everyone who matters to us on an abbreviated trip; or how to meet our ever-enlarging financial needs.

Mental suffering is often due to a specific problem or situation. It often comes from the inability to find an optional or even workable solution when the need for one is intense. It can also be caused by confusion or lack of information regarding something considered vital. This is why so many people suffer when companies restructure. Their ability to provide is up in the air and being decided by someone else.

Spiritual Suffering

> *Pain is God's megaphone.*
> —C. S. LEWIS

Spiritual suffering is often private and hidden. It occurs when we feel adrift, purposeless, hopeless, and unconnected with our universe. Spiritual suffering may take the form of a crisis of faith, the feeling of being utterly insignificant, or the fear that life has no meaning. It can be chronic and vague, like a gnawing sense that something is amiss, or it can be sharp and severe, as when we witness or, worse yet, are victimized by evil—for instance, when we or someone we love is violently and senselessly attacked. We suffer spiritually when our soul is in a state of tumult. Often this is the result of wrestling with big questions that may, in turn, have been sparked by adversities such as the loss of a loved one, a brush with death, or any personally jarring event.

Spiritual suffering also occurs when we know we have fallen short or done wrong on some matter of great importance. It is the chronic hurt that comes from knowing that we let our lower self override our higher self, and, worse yet, that the opportunity to make things right has now passed. It is also often triggered by the most severe stages of the other three kinds of suffering. This may

TYPES OF SUFFERING

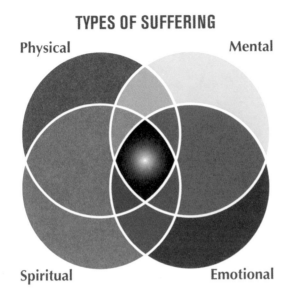

be why so many people consider spiritual suffering to be the most severe, and potentially the most elevating, form.

Do a "Suffer Check"

Whenever things are not going well, experts recommend getting out of the "gray area" as soon as possible. For example, worrying about money problems may make you feel so agitated that it's easier not to think about the problems at all. But then they become a great, gray mist that fills every day with anxiety and uncertainty. The first step to getting out of the financial gray area is figuring out exactly how much money you have and how much you need. Similarly, worrying about a health issue is going to cast a pall over every day and is not going to get you any healthier. Go to the doctor, get a diagnosis, and get out of the gray mist.

If you are suffering due to many different issues at the same time, quantify the amount of suffering you are experiencing with what I call a "suffer check." List all your sources of pain. Start by writing your biggest challenges at the top, and then work your way down from there. Chronic smaller problems can have a wearing effect on your energy, mind, and spirit, so do not hesitate to list them at the bottom of your page, even if they seem trivial. This exercise is a good way of bringing minor upsets out of the shadows.

If you want to be scientific, quantify each problem in terms of its importance, cost, severity, and duration (see below). Give each source of suffering a number from one to ten in all four parameters. This exercise will help you take stock of where you stand, so you can begin to harness suffering for the powerful advantages it can bring.

What Is the Extent of Your Suffering?

Suffering tends to have a cumulative effect, like filling a rain barrel. On a good day, a neighbor's barking dog is a slight annoyance. The level of suffering in your rain barrel goes up only a metaphorical inch. On a bad day, when you are lying in a darkened room suffering from a blinding migraine headache, the barking dog becomes a torment. Added to your headache and any other problems you have, the neighbor's dog causes your rain barrel to overflow.

When you are suffering—physically or mentally—it can be hard to think straight. If you drop an air conditioner on your foot, all you are aware of at first is the pain. You may swear and hop around and maybe cry. After a few moments you may start to wonder if you broke any bones. You wonder if you should go to the doctor, if your health insurance will cover the cost, if you will be able to drive, and so on. If you are a world-class worrier, this accident may quickly balloon into a disaster as you imagine the worst-case scenario: your foot is broken, you'll be on crutches, you'll have to postpone your trip, the X-rays will cost a fortune, and so on.

To keep adversity from ballooning to an overwhelming size, try to put some parameters on your suffering. The more objective you can be in quantifying your pain, the more manageable it becomes. Following are four ways to measure your suffering:

How Important Is This Adversity to You?

The more something matters to you, the more painful it will be when it goes wrong. Let's say you get a cold and lose your voice. For you, this may be an inconvenience. For a soloist at the Metropolitan Opera, this would be a crisis. Ask yourself how much the things you value the most are affected by this setback or challenge. Does it affect your family? Your health? Your job security? Your reputation? Your friendships? Does this adversity affect an area that is trivial in your life, or vital?

What Is the Cost of This Adversity?

This question is related to the first. Define exactly what you are at risk of losing. How high a price will (or may) you be forced to pay, and in what terms? What resources will (or may) you lose? Will the extent of your losses be insignificant, or enormous?

How Severe Is Your Suffering?

Suffering usually implies a hurt of reasonable depth or severity. If something is a mild discomfort, such as a cool room, we don't usually use the word *suffer* unless we're being melodramatic. Do you experience this adversity as practically unnoticeable, or agonizing? How do other people regard your situation?

Suffering is also relative. Ask yourself how severe your pain is compared to those around you, and also in comparison to your previous hardships. When you were young and got stitches for the first time, it probably was a big deal. Let's say you are older and have had stitches a number of times. Now you know the routine, and the same procedure causes less anxiety. A single mother of two who is struggling at a minimum-wage job may genuinely suffer if she loses a twenty-dollar bill. On the other hand, a millionaire who drops a few hundred dollars in a poker game may be unfazed. A child with a splinter may cry out in pain, but a soldier with shrapnel in his leg may weep with relief over surviving such a close call. It all depends on your unique life experiences.

How Long Must You Suffer?

Suffering also can be quantified by duration. Suffering usually implies chronic or protracted discomfort. If something terrible passes quickly, we don't usually apply the word *suffer*. Being hungry for lunch is not suffering. However, being forced to survive a week-long mountain blizzard without enough food is likely to involve real suffering. Is your pain momentary, or long-lasting?

Erik

To Suffer Loss with Love

During the spring of 2004, I spoke at the kickoff event for the Kate Svitek Memorial Foundation near Philadelphia, Pennsylvania. Frank and Ellen Svitek established the foundation to honor their daughter Kate and spread her wish to help people better understand the natural world and the lessons it can teach. The foundation provides financial support to students who, just like Kate, want to explore and discover the outdoors.

Shortly after graduating from college and moving to Bend, Oregon in 2002, Kate was killed in a snowboarding accident while off-duty from her job at Mount Bachelor Ski Resort. Her death was a monumental loss to those who knew her. It completely tore apart a family her parents described as "perfect."

In their invitation to me, Kate's parents said I shared the same outdoor spirit and passion for discovery as their daughter. Having me join them on that special day would help them honor Kate's memory. Traveling to Pennsylvania, I was a little hesitant, because I also shared another part of their story. Only two years after I went blind, my mother was killed in a car accident. This event nearly destroyed me. Compared to the pain of losing my mom, going blind felt almost trivial. The depression I experienced was transformed into a physical suffering. The pain was so intense that I wondered if it could actually cause my heart to stop beating and my blood to stop coursing through my veins. While the pain has subsided a little, the loss remains with me. I carry it in my heart every moment of every day.

So, I had a notion of how a family reacts to the news that a daughter, sister, and friend is gone. I thought to myself, how can two parents be expected to carry on with life when a part of their soul has been ripped from them? And what could I offer this family that could even come close to filling the void in their hearts?

Death, I believe, is the ultimate adversity. Experiencing the death of a loved one is not the same thing as failing on a mountain or losing money on an investment in the stock market; it is adversity to an unfathomable degree. We cannot avoid it, adequately prepare for it, or ever be expected to bounce back from it. The death of a child is something that no parent should ever have to bear. It tests the very nature of the human spirit and our capacity to endure. So how could this ever be considered good suffering?

Kate's mother, Ellen, told me that in the weeks after Kate died, she purposely drove her car without a seat belt, thinking that if she were in an accident, her chances of being with Kate again would be greater. And to this day, Kate's father, Frank, is moved to tears when he shares stories about his daughter. During our conversations, he had to pause repeatedly and fight back tears just to complete a sentence. And when he couldn't, Ellen would complete sentences for him. It made me realize that even today, their suffering is so great that just to endure, Frank and Ellen must live as a single spirit.

I learned that Kate was a passionate climber, and in high school she had attempted Mount Rainier in Washington. In describing her first try, she wrote, "Although, I didn't make it to the summit that sunrise, being near the top of the world gave me a new perspective on life. I realized the importance of challenging one's own limits and ingenuity even if you are not able to achieve a goal. That sunrise placed into me a sense of wonder that had nothing to do with whether or not I made it to the summit. It is not always necessary to achieve an ultimate goal, because the reward of self-satisfaction is enough from within."

Kate's experiences on Mount Rainier had such an impact on her parents that on her second attempt she took her father along as a climbing partner. Even though they fell short of the summit, they made an important discovery—that through physical suffering, the body can do so much more than the brain thinks it can.

Perhaps that discovery led Kate to a third attempt, in which she finally made the summit. And six months after Kate's death, exactly a year after Kate stood on the top of Rainier, her father reached the summit, too. Standing on top in her honor, Frank saw a rainbow. He told me that he believed it was sent by Kate to help him live on.

Frank and Ellen Svitek will suffer intensely the rest of their lives, but, like the rainbow Frank saw above the summit of Rainier, a beautiful and noble calling has arisen from that suffering. In only three years, the foundation has given out almost three dozen scholarships to underprivileged students to attend programs like Outward Bound and the National Outdoor Leadership School. Kate's spirit will live on through the many students who otherwise would not have had the opportunity to follow in her footsteps.

Every night before bed, Kate's mother reads the testimonials from grant recipients and cries. Her suffering is noble, important, and lasting. Nathaly Filion, a grant recipient, wrote, "I have learned so much about myself, the natural world, and my passion for the outdoors. I thank you from the bottom of my heart."

Frank and Ellen's sadness could have easily grown into a noxious weed. Who would have blamed them if they had become bitter and withdrawn? By finding a purpose to their pain, instead, it blossomed into a fragrant flower and shows us what it means to suffer with love.

Paul

How to Suffer Poorly

When you suffer genuine physical, emotional, mental, and/or spiritual pain, who could ever blame you for checking out, being miserable, and making everyone else miserable in the process? Who could judge you for subtracting from the world through your suffering? After all, you're *suffering*!

Unfortunately, suffering can be the ultimate excuse to stop trying. Bad suffering occurs when the experience makes us less, rather than more, and when we bring others down, rather than elevate them. When we become meaner, smaller, or more selfish as a result of our pain, that is bad suffering, even if it is understandable. If we hurt ourselves, or hurt others because we hurt, we are suffering poorly. When we reduce our Life Worth and the Life Worth of those around us because of our pain, we are suffering less nobly than we perhaps could. When the net effect of our suffering is that we have damaged the belief and faith of others, we have, indeed, suffered badly.

Sometimes suffering becomes a cultural norm within organizations. I'll never forget one senior vice president who said to me,

"In case you haven't noticed, Paul, these changes are not *fun*. In fact, nothing about our company is *fun*. Just surviving in business these days is damned tough. So, I suggest you put your optimism aside. Just help us work through the grim realities of this situation, and stop trying to convince us how wonderful change can be." Needless to say, the hallways of this company were filled with the walking dead, and their competitors beat them with the buzz, energy, excitement, and innovation that drove real numbers.

There are entirely human coping mechanisms that we all indulge in when we are confronted with adversity. We all use them, with the best of intentions, but they can become destructive. Done to excess or too often, they interfere with our ability to suffer well. The purpose of this book is not to coddle you, but to *strengthen* you, so read the following with that purpose in mind.

Going Nowhere: Whining and Complaining

Most people despise other people's whining, even if they love to complain themselves. Whining brings to mind a tired child at the toy store, relentlessly pleading for a treat despite dogged resistance from the parent.

Whining and complaining usually go hand-in-hand with passiveness. The whiner is venting, and waiting for someone else to do something about his or her problem. People who whine often don't have enough drive to do anything about their plight, yet their capacity for complaining never flags.

The problem with whining and complaining is that, overdone, it makes us weak. A bad attitude can be highly contagious. When you let loose on all the things you're unhappy about, you invite everyone else to do the same. People don't leave a team complaint session energized and exuberant. Instead, they leave depressed.

Raising a legitimate concern is usually not considered whining. When leaders say, "There's an awful lot of whining going on right now," they are implying that, from their perspective, the complaints are out of line.

Suffering is not the same as whining. If your spouse just cleared out the bank account and left you forever, or informed you that he (or she) is having an affair, or switched sexual orientation, you are entitled to talk about it because you are suffering. Whining applies to the smaller stuff. No one wants to hear you whine about the line at the grocery store, your parking ticket, your cell phone service, or your veterinarian bill, because being inconvenienced is not the same as suffering.

Sometimes we need to express our unhappiness about something in order to come to grips with it and get past it. Putting a constructive spin on your observations will help you steer clear of empty complaints and hone your determination.

Trying to Hide: Escaping and Blaming

"You can run, but you can't hide" is the warning label that should accompany all suffering. Suffering is like a heat-seeking missile. No matter how far you run, or how creatively you hide, suffering and its lessons will somehow find you.

I see businesses trying to hide their fatal flaws in more and more growth, but the truth always catches up. For example, one business had significant flaws in its new "flagship technology," but instead of fixing it, they sold it aggressively and let the nightmares rain down on tech support. Once the bubble bursts, the blame game begins, and responsibility for the disaster is tossed around like a hot potato.

When you blame others, you shift responsibility off your shoulders. This may help you sleep at night, and it may help you preserve your self-esteem, but when you give up responsibility, you also give up control—and along with it, your power to fix what went wrong. When you blame others, you miss out on a vital piece of your own development. Playing the victim ensures that you won't learn or grow from your experience.

It is normal to try to escape hardship. But it is more powerful and courageous to enter the storm, embrace the challenge, and harness its cleansing force. Sometimes we have to let adversity sandblast our souls. Perhaps the greatest lesson in this book is this: *do not fear suffering*. Rather than trying to escape adversity, or trying to shield yourself from blame, live your life on a grand scale and take what comes.

Identifying: Letting Your Suffering Define Who You Are

Sometimes we can get too close to our suffering. This is what happens when the cancer patient unconsciously comes to need her cancer, because it has become the source for long-overdue attention and love. It's what happens when people have labels, like "that one-armed guy," "that stage mother," "that genius kid," and so on. Terms like "recovering alcoholic" and "disabled" are identifiers. They provide a sort of shorthand for understanding another person's condition, and they provide a sense of belonging with others who share a similar label. The problem arises when a label moves from being a *description* to being a *definition* that limits our understanding of the whole person. To define Erik as "the blind guy who climbed Everest" is to completely ignore Erik the successful husband, father, son, speaker, charitable leader, and businessman.

As a first step, we need to modify our language so that the person comes first, not the condition. You may privately think of your neighbor as "Crazy Carl," but it makes a difference when you refer to him as "Carl, who has a condition called bipolar disorder." Saying "cancer victim Gina" defines Gina as a sick person, while "Gina, who is living with cancer" makes it clear that Gina is a human being who exists separately from her illness. Instead of describing yourself as a depressive, say, "I experience episodes of depression." Maintaining your independence from your suffering allows you to prevail over it.

Rationalizing Away the Need to Change

The human capacity to come up with rational explanations is boundless. This is how we make sense of the world, and studies have shown that the human brain will go to great lengths not just to *recognize* order and meaning, but also to *create* them even where they don't exist. We can explain or rationalize almost anything, from being late to an appointment, to weighing a couple of pounds more than usual, to finding a slip of paper with a mysterious phone number in our partner's pocket. Sometimes rationalizing gives us hope. But our persuasive powers work against us when we use them to insulate ourselves from reality, and to disguise our unwillingness to become better people.

One of Erik's friends recently showed his genius for rationalizing when he said, "I imagine you must just possess some superhuman gene for suffering. I know for sure that I don't, so I could *never* deal with the kind of pain *you* do, or accomplish the kinds of things you accomplish. You're obviously some sort of genetic aberration [nice word for *freak*]."

Erik responded by gently pointing out, "Actually, I'm just like you. Whatever capacity for suffering you think I have is really the long-term result of the decisions I've made and the challenges I've chosen to take on. There's nothing I'm doing, in my way, that you could not do in an equivalent way of your own. That's the whole point of my message: to shatter people's perceptions of what's possible."

Painting a Pretty Picture: Pretending and Whitewashing

Pretending takes denial one step further. It is acting as though what we know exists does not exist. The child with a cookie in his hand, standing next to the cookie jar, will pretend he has no idea where that cookie came from. When we get caught pretending, we look just as silly and a lot less cute.

Whitewashing is the handmaiden of pretending. The term is based on covering flaws with a layer of cheap white paint. Think of Tom Sawyer whitewashing that fence. It's also related to the "white lie." Whitewashing is an attempt to make things seem better than they really are—embellishing a résumé, for example, or telling a prospective buyer that the basement is "damp" when in fact it floods once a year. Advertising, public relations, marketing, and political careers all involve expertise in whitewashing.

Putting a positive spin on things can serve a useful purpose—for example, research shows that smiling, even when we least feel like it, can create healthful changes within our bodies. Sometimes "fake it 'til you make it" provides just enough motivation to move you in a positive direction. Most often, however, pretending and whitewashing are used to deceive others.

The inducement to pretend can be tremendous. When a project is in trouble, pretending that everything is "going great" will keep the boss calm, and buy you time to figure out a solution. But what happens when the boss eventually finds out the truth? How likely is he or she to believe your next status report? When you pretend to your family that everything is financially solid when it is not, how long will it take until you are found out, and what lessons will others take away from this deception? As a good friend whose mother is suffering from breast cancer explains, "Every time I call, my mother tells me she's doing pretty well, getting along okay, and not worrying too much. She never tells me how scared she feels, or what the doctors *really* say about her situation. Here she is, going through the biggest challenge of her life, and I've never felt so distant. It's like she's put a veil over the whole thing. And it's driving me nuts!"

Pretending and whitewashing create barriers between us and other people. When we pretend everything is great, we deny others the lessons and experience our suffering can offer them. When others whitewash our suffering, they withhold their connection from us and deny us the opportunity to suffer well with them. Suffering well is incompatible with any form of deception, however harmless it is intended to be.

Suffering? What Suffering? Anesthetizing and Denying

Understandably, people often try to anesthetize themselves against pain. Sometimes this is as straightforward as swapping pills for pain. Some people escape by using recreational drugs, sex, alcohol, pornography, television, video games, or the Internet. I see people of all ages anesthetizing themselves against the hardships of school or work through a variety of readily available numbing devices. The suffering caused by an unbearable home life or excruciating divorce can be numbed—consciously or unconsciously—by a workaholic lifestyle. I see a disconcerting number of executives who rely more and more on the adrenaline rush of their day jobs as a way to offset harsh realities at home.

When we feel no pain, it's easier to deny that there are problems that need to be addressed. The temptation to deny is immense. It is far easier to look the other way than to deal with your problems head-on. It is easier to delude yourself that your job (life, marriage, family, health) is going great than to shine a bright light on the situation and do the work necessary to repair the cracks.

Denial is not a judgment. It is a relationship. We are "in denial" when we fail to completely accept the full magnitude of our adversity and the extent of its consequences. Culture plays a powerful role here. For example, the British are known for keeping a "stiff upper lip" no matter what they may be feeling or experiencing. Theirs is not the only culture that believes one should suffer with quiet dignity (think Scandinavian, Asian). This kind of stoicism and the need to keep up appearances is often accompanied by denial.

Numbing the pain of your circumstances and denying the full extent of your problems can be temporarily useful, if your suffering is overwhelming. But hiding your eyes does not make the tiger disappear. My recommendation is to be as open and candid about your suffering as you can. Ask for help when you need it. You can even turn your suffering into a cause. Let others learn from what you are going through. We're all human, and I believe we're here to help and learn from each other.

How to Suffer Well

*Suffering, cheerfully endured, ceases to be suffering
and is transmuted into an ineffable joy.*
— MAHATMA GANDHI

The result of suffering well is making yourself a better person, and the people around you better people. Suffering poorly is your right. Suffering well is your opportunity.

Suffering well can press the personal "reset" button. It clears everything superfluous off our radar screen. Good suffering often involves some sort of catharsis, where the pain we endure brings with it exceptional clarity about what really matters, and impatience with focusing on anything less. It sweeps us clean of pettiness, making us more magnanimous and selfless.

Suffering well cannot be done in isolation. Research reveals a somewhat inverse relationship between happiness and self-absorption. Getting outside your own skin and focusing on others, especially in times of suffering, can reduce your pain and create some upside to what is otherwise a down experience. When we suffer well, we transcend our pain in an effort to make life better for others. We help them believe that, whatever they must some-day endure, it does not have to end horribly. By seeing you suffer well, they begin to believe that they can, too.

Following are eight steps that will help you shift your hardship to suffering well:

1. *Identify the one area in which you currently suffer the most.* This provides the greatest opportunity for transforming adversity into elevation. You have already determined your Summit Adversity, so you can go directly to the next step!

2. *Ask yourself who is most affected by the manner in which you suffer.* The answer might not be obvious. Beyond those closest to you, there may be people in the next ring of family, friends, and associates who are profoundly affected by your situation, and their lives may be changed by your approach. Suffer well by expressing in words and deeds your brand of appreciation, beauty, love, gratitude, faith, or wisdom to others, especially when your pain is most intense.

3. *Clarify in your own mind why it is important that you suffer well.* Without a compelling reason, chances are you won't be successful. You may know people who have been able to endure terrible difficulties by focusing on a compelling goal or reason. It can literally keep people alive. Think about the people you know, the people who might someday experience what you are experiencing, the legacy you choose to leave, and your personal dignity. Put into one sentence your rallying reason for taking it on. "Rather than suffer poorly, I choose to Suffer Well because . . ."

4. *Engage your CORE (from Summit Three).* Determine how much Control you have (can you influence the situation?); how you can take Ownership (can you think of a way to step up and make a

positive improvement?); the Reach of the adversity (what can you do to minimize the downside, and maximize the potential upside?); and how much Endurance will be required (how quickly can you expect to get past this?).

5. *Think about what you want life to look like on the other side.* As a result of your commitment, what benefits should you and the people around you enjoy? Spend some time imagining the most positive outcome possible. What you imagine may become real.

6. *Review the types of behavior that interfere with suffering well.* These include Whining and Complaining, Escaping and Blaming, Identifying, Rationalizing, Pretending and Whitewashing, and Anesthetizing and Denying. Which of these are problem areas for you? Which can you commit yourself to stopping, or at least minimizing?

7. *Create a timeline.* By when will you have said or done something that demonstrates your commitment to suffering well? Time takes on a new dimension when you are suffering. Scheduling a goal is often a powerful way to help you endure the short term. Commit yourself to accomplishing one specific thing by a certain date or time. This can be highly motivating and can help your body and spirit rally for the cause.

8. *Discuss your conclusions with the people who are most involved with your situation.*

Their understanding, support, and involvement benefit not only you, but them as well.

> *Suffering becomes beautiful when anyone bears calamities with cheerfulness, not through insensibility but through greatness of mind.*
> —ARISTOTLE

Erik

Carstensz

The necessary and even healthy role of suffering is understandable in theory, but when I experienced it firsthand on my eighth summit, it was bitter medicine. Although 7,310-foot Kosciuszko is the tallest peak on the mainland of Australia, many geographers consider the true seventh summit to be an extremely remote peak 2,400 miles to the north, on the island of New Guinea. Others place this peak on an eighth continent called Oceania. Carstensz Pyramid—or Mbaigela, in the local Moni language—is a jagged and snowcapped peak that looms 16,023 feet above the vast central rain forest and tops out with a 2,000-foot wall of limestone.

The local tribes near the mountain are some of the most primitive on earth, still using stone tools and wearing nothing but penis gourds called *kotekas* held on by rattan cords tied around their waists. Until forty years ago, they still practiced ritualistic cannibalism on their enemies. Carstensz was at the top of my "to-do" list, but for many years an independence movement, combined with an extremely secretive international gold mine on the south side of the mountain, made the entire region very unstable and off-limits to outsiders. In 2005, a group of university students from Jakarta trekking through the jungle were kidnapped and hacked to pieces by the local rebels. Only recently has the area been opened again to climbers.

For me, the indisputable crux of the journey wasn't the climb itself, but the approach. A new route to Base Camp had recently been forged from the small village of Sugapa, where we landed in a supply plane crammed with climbing gear for us, and with pigs for the locals. We learned we would be only the third group to make this approach—seven days and fifty miles through one of the densest rain forests in the world.

Only faint hunting and game trails existed, so we weaved and bobbed, with Lucas, our head porter, in front of us, hacking away at the vegetation with his machete. Describing it as "walking" would be misleading. More

Charley Mace and I pose with our local Moni porters before setting off for a difficult seven-day slog through the New Guinea rain forest to Carstensz Pyramid. The local tribespeople represent a clash between old and new worlds. Penis gourds and bow and arrows contrast with camouflage and M16s.

often we crawled on our hands and knees in the deep mud, through narrow slots under fallen trees, and then along the tops of those trees, since their knobby trunks were usually the only open pathways. I learned quickly that jungles are far from flat. The ground is so soft that powerful rivers cut deep, narrow valleys through the earth, which we had to cross. Often we had to climb hundreds of feet up slippery moss and roots, or sidehill along minuscule trails that dropped away on one side into a white raging river. My longtime climbing partner, Charley Mace, would look down and always say the same thing: "E, this is a *don't fall* zone."

Our second partner was Hans Florine, regarded as one of the fastest climbers in the world. Hans climbed El Capitan, a 3,300-foot rock face in Yosemite Valley, in 157 minutes. The same route took me three days. With Hans in front talking me through the forest, I commented on the irony of the fastest climber in the world guiding the slowest. Frequently, we'd scramble for hours over chaotic latticeworks of exposed roots rising up twenty feet or more off the ground. My trekking poles, which I lean on for balance, would constantly pop through the gaps and send me flailing. I was so envious of the locals who walked casually along with their bare toes gripping the gnarled roots like fingers. Occasionally the flora would open up enough that we actually got to walk upright, but at the same time we were usually squishing through knee-deep mud, my poles continually sinking and getting stuck nearly to the handles. Even so, simply being vertical was enough to feel like a weight had been lifted from my shoulders.

The irony was that I had chosen to be here. I had completed the traditional version of the Seven Summits. Carstensz was an add-on. The second and even greater irony was that we'd had the option of taking a helicopter straight to the mountain's base, skipping the difficult jungle approach altogether. But flying over the rain forest and bagging a peak, with the least amount of inconvenience, didn't sit right with me. I wanted to fully experience this place, and I realized that would require suffering. This made perfect sense before we actually started. In the midst of the groveling, though, part of me couldn't stop asking what I was doing here.

The river crossings might have been the toughest part. Bridges were a couple of trees laid across the torrent, lashed together by rattan vines. I'd inch across as the tree trunks wobbled and swayed, with Lucas walking backward, holding tight to my wrists. On river crossings where no bridges were built, Charley and Hans would talk me through, banging their trekking poles against the rocks where I was supposed to hop. Our porters got a kick out of this exercise and began to make a game of it. They'd close their eyes and try to hop across the rivers. Sometimes I'd hear a splash, followed by roars of laughter.

On the fourth day, I slipped on a wet, smooth pile of river rocks, landing so hard on my hand I couldn't feel my fingers and couldn't grip the roots and trees to climb. I already had bruises and festering scrapes covering my shins, elbows, and hands from a dozen other falls. I worried about the next slip. If I broke my leg, getting back through the impenetrable forest would be a horrendous epic. Even worse, I knew I was slowing up Hans and Charley, jeopardizing their chance for success. That was hard to bear. Our rations didn't allow for indecision, so we had to keep pushing. It was another twelve hours before we found just enough of a flat spot to set up camp. The porters quickly cut down small bamboo trees and constructed a lean-to. When we were finally resting, Charley looked at his altimeter and sadly noted that with all the ascending and descending of that day, we'd gained only 300 feet of overall elevation; the mountain was still a long way above us.

I was beat-up and demoralized from the unrelenting terrain. To make matters worse, little sunlight made it through the thick canopy, giving the rain forest an oppressive and claustrophobic quality. As a blind guy, I appreciated the open feel of high mountains where wind could blow and sound could carry over distances, but in the jungle, sounds were closed-in and muffled. I felt depressed, even a little panicky and short of breath, like I was trapped and would never escape from the jungle's grasp.

I'd been doing my utmost to tough it out in silence, but the words that had been building all day spilled out of me: "What if I can't make it? What if this is too much for me?"

Like most climbers, Charley is a very blunt guy. Once while skiing in

Alaska, I asked him how my form looked. "Like a train wreck," he replied without a trace of humor. But outside our tent, Charley put his hand on my shoulder and said, "E, you've been working your butt off, and I know how hard this is. But you're a good man, and good things happen to good people. We'll get through this." His words were exactly what I needed, and for several minutes I couldn't speak. Then Hans called out from his tent with his customary good night: "Thanks, E, for bringing me on this awesome camping trip!" We all burst out laughing.

The next morning, as usual, we wrung out our soaking-wet socks, stuffed them into filthy, waterlogged boots, and started another twelve hours of stumbling and thrashing. Hans was having fun with the tedium of the terrain. "Slippery mud, roots, and rocks ahead," he called, and a minute later, "slippery rocks, mud, and roots ahead," and still later, "Lots of mud, roots, and rocks—careful—very slippery." Despite my exhaustion, I'd smile each time. Charley would often stop and describe the colors of the rain forest, an explosion of orchids—blues, whites, and purples contrasted by a backdrop of deep green; I could see it clearly in my mind. I made myself pause to explore with my hands the fat rough palm trees with giant bulbs like bird nests called *sarang semut,* and the variety of jungle fruits. My favorite—like a small, smooth coconut—was called *pakees.* I marveled over the banana leaves, as wide as my spread arms, and every now and then we were rewarded by the enchanting call of a mynah bird.

When we stopped for lunch on the trail, the porters would build small, smoky brushfires, and we'd sit around trying to learn local Moni words, the porters howling with laughter each time we butchered their language. I traded bites of candy bars for their roasted yams, and Lucas even let me shoot his bow and arrow. On our seventh day, the labyrinth finally began to give way, and I felt small patches of sun touch my face. I was so relieved, tears welled up in my eyes. But the sun was short-lived. We arrived in Base Camp drenched and shivering in a torrential rainstorm.

Finally in my tent, I allowed myself to rest. I had embarked on this trip with ingrained notions of who I was and how I related to the world, but the jungle had grabbed hold of my ego and stripped it away, through a dozen

After the punishing jungle approach, we set out for Carstensz Pyramid's summit at 2 AM. To get to the top, we had to cross a Tyrolean traverse, a line suspended in the air connecting two ridges.

stubborn layers and right down to the naked bone. The hardships had left me as vulnerable as a small child, yet what remained felt more open and honest—a child's wonderment of beautiful things, a child's implicit trust, and a child's unique ability to give and receive love. The oozing mud, the pouring rain, and the exhaustion of twelve-hour days had not destroyed me. Instead they had released me. In their own torturous way, these miseries were as poignant as the summit itself. In fact, it was the jungle that gave the summit its significance.

We celebrated our arrival at Base Camp the next morning with a numbing bath in a nearby mountain lake. As a reward to me for making it, Lucas took off his prized necklace of shells and dried orchid stems and tied it around my neck. Our summit day went off without a hitch. At 2 AM, we started up the trail, climbed the steep face, and carefully traversed along a narrow and convoluted ridge—crossing over patches of ice and snow. At 7:34 in the morning, I stepped on to my eighth summit with Charley and Hans.

"I wouldn't be here without you two," I said. Hans leaned in and gave me a giant hug. His voice catching, he called out, "Thanks, E, for this awesome camping trip."

I will never forget the suffering I went through in the rain forest of New Guinea, and I would certainly never wish myself back there. However, knowing what I do now, I would not have missed the jungle for the world. For me, the question isn't *why* we suffer, but *how*. Does our pain turn into poison, or do we suffer with humility and grace? Does it clamp our minds shut to the fullness of experience, or can we convert our anguish into something meaningful, which has the chance to lift up others? For me, I always return to the same question: In the face of daunting challenge, did I suffer well?

By the way, the next morning we called from our satellite phone and arranged a helicopter for the trip out. I'm all for suffering well, but I'm no masochist.

Deliver Greatness, Every Day

MOUNT KILIMANJARO

Base Camp: 3,000 feet
Summit: 19,300 feet
Located in Tanzania, Mount Kilimanjaro is the tallest peak in Africa.

We give others the courage to do great things
by our own example of doing great things.

–STEVE ACKERMAN, THE FIRST PARAPLEGIC TO
PEDAL AROUND THE WORLD ON A HAND CYCLE

ROUTE DESCRIPTION

- ▶ Everyday Greatness
- ▶ Your Role Model
- ▶ Your Everyday Greatness Game Plan
  - • Summit One: Take It On! . . . Summit Two: Summon Your Strengths . . . Summit Three: Engage Your CORE . . . Summit Four: Pioneer Possibilities . . . Summit Five: Pack Light, Pack Right . . . Summit Six: Suffer Well . . . Crafting Your Game Plan
- ▶ Putting Greatness into Action
- ▶ Blindsight

Erik

I've climbed Kilimanjaro twice now, and the contrast between my two very different ascents helped me discover that there's much more to life than standing proudly on top of the mountain and declaring to the world, "Look at me! I did it!" I learned that success means more than overcoming immense physical obstacles, such as extreme cold and fierce winds. It means helping others transform their own challenges into triumphs.

I organized the first trip to Kilimanjaro in 1997 as my second continental summit, but equally important, to give my father, Ed, and my wife, Ellie, a taste of bigger mountains. I wanted them to experience the same joy of climbing that I did, and I thought Kilimanjaro would be the perfect setting. However, I didn't do my homework or plan properly, as I learned to do on later expeditions. Instead I hired a local guide, who turned out to be less than reliable. He rushed us up the mountain, so that everyone became sick from the altitude. On the night before our summit attempt, he had us camp too low on the mountain, which made for a hellishly long summit day. His plan required covering 5,000 feet to the summit and 8,000 feet down in twenty hours—a feat that certainly took a toll on our team. As we ascended, some people moved faster than others, so the team quickly got spread across the mountain into isolated groups, none of which knew what the others were doing.

Before reaching the summit, a woman in the group ahead of us curled up in a ball and refused to move. "Just let me die!" she repeated to her horrified guides, who had to haul her down. When the mountain flattened out, they actually had to lay her on a wheeled gurney used to carry fresh game.

A guy in our team was so wasted that on the endless descent he began giving away all his climbing gear, repeating to anyone he passed, "This is a terrible sport. I'm never climbing again."

One of our assistant guides was wearing sunglasses with lenses too dark to see through. He kept having to take them off, and eventually got retinal burns from the intense sun. He stumbled around, practically blind and in intense pain, with white pus oozing from the corners of his eyes.

The worst part of the climb came on the crater rim, only an hour below the top, when my dad and Ellie both decided to turn back. "Are you having a good time?" I asked Ellie, dreading the answer. "No," she said. "This is an endless nightmare."

Although I suffered from altitude sickness and was stopping every thirty feet in the last hour to throw up, I toughed it out and reached the summit. I had surmounted the adversity and achieved my goal. Good for me. So why, then, did I feel like I had failed? Because the two people I loved the most in the world were somewhere below me. Were they okay, or were they suffering? Were they lost? Were they hurt? I had talked them into this climb, and when it really mattered, I hadn't used my strengths to help them or encourage them on, as others had done for me. I was standing on top, but it was a bitter success. Instead of celebrating, I cried.

Eight years later, I began corresponding with an extraordinary athlete named Douglas Sidialo. He lived in Nairobi, Kenya, with his wife and two daughters. In 1998, Douglas was driving past the American Embassy when he witnessed a flash of light. That was the last thing he ever saw. He woke up in the hospital three days later having lost both eyes, an innocent casualty of the simultaneous bombings by Al-Qaeda of the U.S. embassies in Kenya and Tanzania.

In Africa, blind people are hardly ever employed. So Douglas and his family had to survive on his wife's small teaching salary. When Douglas told me his dream was to climb Kilimanjaro someday as a way to spread a message of peace throughout the world, I couldn't sleep for the next three nights. My brain churned with an adventure that might help Douglas and his family, and possibly many others, too.

The plan sprang from the knowledge of two opposing experiences: the emptiness of my first Kilimanjaro summit, and the joy I experienced on Mount Everest when so many of my team members stood on top with me. I

PHOTOGRAPH BY ELLEN WEIHENMAYER

The first time I reached the top of Kilimanjaro, my wife and father turned back below the summit. Although I toughed it out and made the top, it was a bitter success. I returned almost ten years later committed to doing it right, leading a team of blind and sighted climbers from four continents.

attributed our crowded Everest summit to everyone's desire to be a part of something great. That commitment and loyalty drove us all to the summit. I suspected that the same magic could be replicated on Kilimanjaro.

I decided to form a team of sighted and blind participants—not elite athletes, but everyday people like stay-at-home moms, corporate folks, and weekend warriors. Ninety percent of the sighted participants were flatlanders from places like Boston, Mobile, and Tokyo. Most had little mountaineering experience, and half were middle-aged and older. Their job would be to guide the blind people to the top. Besides Douglas, the blind participants included people from four continents. Just to make things interesting, we also brought along Carl, a visually impaired and hearing-impaired participant from Denver, and Bill, who was sixty-nine years old, and who not only was blind, but also was missing part of his right arm and some fingers from his left hand from a blasting accident in Alaska.

For the first step, I brought the team to Colorado for a training hike to hone our systems and build team strengths. Since most of the sighted members were novices at guiding blind people, everyone struggled to figure out how to best work with everyone else. Instead of taking the standard six hours, our training hike took twelve hours, and only two blind people actually made it to the top. But by sticking it out together, the team members had shown they had the will to do something great.

When we reassembled in Africa, the sighted and blind partners came prepared with new guiding systems they had developed. Some duos held opposite ends of two trekking poles. With others, the blind person lightly held a strap on a backpack. In another case, the sighted person rang a bear bell for his blind partner to follow.

At the base of Kilimanjaro, I told the group this climb was not just about getting a few individuals to the summit. The end goal was to summit as a team, and to take care of one another each step of the way.

Our first test came only two days into the trek as one of our blind climbers was struggling through the endless boulder fields before camp. Three teammates stayed behind to help him through. The African guides offered to carry him into camp, but the team tenaciously refused. The small group finally came into camp late that evening, after a twelve-hour day, and the folks who had arrived earlier already had tents set up, sleeping bags laid out, and a hot meal waiting.

Higher up on the Barranco Wall—a steep, 1,000-foot rock scramble—I listened to my sighted teammates working patiently and carefully to help Douglas through every step. As I knew very well, one wrong move meant a 200-foot slide.

On summit night, everyone snaked up the headwall in a long line. We moved as a single unit. Not one person sprinted ahead to the summit. By early morning, as the team finally crested the headwall and stood at Gilman's Point—still an hour below the true summit—people were exhausted. One team member was close to passing out over his ski pole. Another was seeing double, and a third had sprained his ankle and limped painfully with every step. I knew that some were barely hanging on, and said to the team, "I think we should call it good and stop here." I was immediately and unanimously overruled, and an hour later we all stood on the Roof of Africa.

Life at 19,000 feet is rough. You struggle for every breath. Your brain aches, and your heart pounds against your chest. Normally, a large proportion of people get sick of the pain and discomfort and call it quits. But, to my delight, my theory proved true. By having an important purpose, we got twenty-three out of twenty-seven to the top, far more than anyone would have expected.

On our last night on the mountain, teammate Paul Polman stood up at dinner and announced, "We've had such a rewarding experience together, one that none of us will ever forget. Our climb together is now coming to an end, but I propose we create a lasting legacy of our time together." The result was the Kilimanjaro Blind Trust, which the team formed to improve Braille literacy for blind children throughout East Africa. In three years of operation, the foundation has worked in dozens of schools for the blind, repairing and replacing hundreds of broken Braillers—the machines used by blind teachers and students to type Braille.

In my climbing career, I've climbed many higher mountains and many

PHOTOGRAPH BY CHARLEY MACE

The highlight of my second Kilimanjaro expedition was reaching the summit with my friend Douglas Sidialo, who became the first blind African to stand on the roof of his continent.

harder mountains, but few gave me the same sense of fulfillment as helping a blind African to stand on the roof of his continent for the first time. We did more than surmount adversity that day. We used it to elevate the entire team, and, through the trust, to improve the quality of life for hundreds of blind students for years to come.

By the way, Douglas must have gotten hooked on adventuring, because the next year, he, along with his buddy, rode my donated tandem bike 7,500 miles, north to south, Cairo to Cape Town, and became the first blind man to cycle the length of Africa. Today Douglas speaks around the world on moving beyond conflict and strife to unite as one people.

Paul

Everyday Greatness

There is a fundamental difference between the greatness of the historic figures whose biographies fill the library shelves, and the kind of greatness we are exploring together here. It's like the difference between looking skyward to some distant, daunting, windblown peak, and looking at a steep hill in your own backyard. This book is not so much about the accomplishment of a single epic event, but about the pursuit of everyday greatness through ongoing effort and everyday opportunity.

Most people are not striving to be Abraham Lincoln, Nelson Mandela, or Gandhi—the kind of larger-than-life individuals who rise up and do the right thing in the face of immense adversity, changing the course of human history in the process. But we all strive to have our lives matter, to close our eyes for the final time knowing that even a small piece of the world is better for our having been here.

The book *Slow Man*, by Nobel Prize–winning author J. M. Coetzee, tells the story of a man who near the end of his life realizes that while he has done little significant harm in his life, he has done no good, either. He will leave no trace behind . . . he has slid through the world without making any difference. He imagines arriving at the pearly gates and being asked: "Did you not understand why you were given life, the greatest gift of all?"

Everyday greatness is like charity. Which is the more heartfelt contribution: the millionaire cutting a tax-deductible check, or the child emptying her piggy bank? Which demonstrates more strength of character: elevating others when you are healthy, wealthy, and wise, or doing so while you are suffering? The virtues of everyday greatness include resilience, magnanimity, compassion, fortitude, goodwill, and integrity. Leaders deliver these readily and generously, not just when life is good, but even when they are being slammed against the rocks. If it were easy, we would call it "everyday normality" instead of everyday greatness.

Your Role Model

Everyday greatness is not generic, but rather highly individualized. You deliver your brand of everyday greatness in your own unique and authentic way—and others do, too. If you are looking for a way to get started, consider the people you admire in your life, at work, at school, or in your community. Narrow the field down to one person. What does that person do, or demonstrate, that makes him or her worthy of your admiration? As you reflect upon this person, analyze his or her character in terms of the chapters you have just read:

From Summit One, "Take It On!":
▶ Where do you believe this person falls on the Adversity Continuum?
▶ What adversity has this person taken on?
▶ What assumptions do you think this person makes about adversity?

From Summit Two, "Summon Your Strengths":

▶ What is the toughest or most important challenge you've seen this person take on?

▶ What skills does he or she exhibit during adversity?

▶ Of these, which do you most admire?

▶ Are you aware of any evidence that this person went outside his or her comfort zone to develop new strengths to meet adversity?

▶ How strong would you rate this person's will?

▶ Does he or she work with a team?

▶ How do other members of the team complement this person's strengths?

From Summit Three, "Engage Your CORE":

▶ How would you rate this person's ability to respond to adversity (AQ)?

▶ To what extent does he or she engage his or her CORE? (You will recall that Control is the ability to focus on what can be influenced, Ownership is the willingness to step up and make a positive difference, Reach is all about containing adversity, and Endurance is being able to get past adverse events.)

▶ Have you ever seen this person use Energy Lending by imagining and pursuing a positive outcome?

From Summit Four, "Pioneering Possibilities":

▶ How does this person respond when someone says something important is impossible?

▶ Is there anything impossible that this person has made possible?

▶ Have you seen this person devise and use any innovative Signature Systems to handle adversity?

From Summit Five, "Pack Light, Pack Right":

▶ How much does this person care about "stuff"?

▶ Can you think of an instance when this person has turned down a gain in net worth for a gain in Life Worth?

- How effectively does he or she strategically invest time, energy, and money in the things that matter most?
- How does this person treat other people?
- Does this person invest in his or her own physical, mental, emotional, and spiritual well-being?

From Summit Six, "Suffer Well":
- What physical, mental, emotional, or spiritual suffering have you seen this person endure?
- How does this person handle pain and suffering?
- How likely are you to find this person whining, complaining, blaming, identifying, anesthetizing, escaping, rationalizing, denying, pretending, or whitewashing?
- What is this person's relationship with drugs, alcohol, and other forms of escapism?
- What effect does his or her approach have on others?

You may wish to jot down your answers to these questions, or even go through the exercise again with others to gain additional insights. While everyone is different, there are powerful similarities among those people who handle adversity successfully. It doesn't matter if they are famous or unknown; they all manage to maintain noble ambitions while facing significant adversity. Ultimately, through struggle and suffering, they elevate themselves and others, turning the adversity into a meaningful advantage.

In the introduction, I explained that Erik is the exemplar of everything this book is about, and I told you that my intention was to decode his emotional DNA so that you could go and replicate it inside yourself, in your own way, for your Summit Challenge and your life. Now I suggest that you repeat the exercise above, applying the same questions to Erik, based on what you have learned about him from this book. I am not going to provide the answers for you, because your challenge in this final chapter is to make sure you fully understand the Adversity Advantage. While it would be easy to distance yourself from Erik, considering him to be a superhuman mutation, he is in fact a regular guy who did something you or anyone can do: use adversity to your advantage. You can replicate in your life, with your adversities, all the ways Erik turned lead into gold.

If you're interested, you could repeat the same exercise a third time, using the person you most admire in the entire span of human history. Your answers probably will bear an enormous similarity to those you've already given. In all likelihood the people you admire most, from any century or walk of life, are adept at harnessing adversity, and they earn your respect, trust, and admiration by demonstrating the principles of this book in their daily lives.

Now that you have reviewed the common practices, principles, and tools of the high-AQ people you most admire, here is a final and most important question: *Of all the characteristics you identified during this exercise, which ones would you NOT be able to re-create and put to use within yourself and within your own life?* I hope your answer is: none!

Your Everyday Greatness Game Plan

The time has come for you to create your master plan. Your goal is to ascend to the top of the Adversity Continuum, where—by suffering well—you will be able to turn misfortune and adversity into innovation and opportunities. It doesn't matter if your adversity is large (for example, a crisis like going blind) or small (for example, an annoyance at work): the principles of harnessing adversity are effective on all levels.

Your Everyday Greatness Game Plan is both portable and personal. You may choose to track your progress through your weekly planner. You may decide to share the journey with others, including loved ones, coworkers, and colleagues, creating your own rope team by holding each other accountable for the commitments you make. Or you may simply have a weekly cup of coffee to share your progress, discoveries, and challenges with your best friend. Whether private or shared, your Everyday Greatness Game Plan will help you and the people around you benefit from adversity.

There are two possible pathways. If you choose the *Singular Challenge*, you will focus on your Summit Challenge—the one thing you've always wanted to do but have not done. The benefit of this approach is being able to concentrate on success in one area. The second possibility is the *Multiple Challenge*, when you apply the same principles and tools to those pains or adversities that you listed under each Life Category in your Adversity Inventory in Summit One. If you take this approach, you will have lots of ideas for turning each of these adversities to your advantage. The benefit of this approach is its breadth. It potentially covers most of the facets of your life.

How do you decide which approach is best for you? I would suggest you consider the source of your greatest pain, and potential fulfillment. If not having accomplished your Summit Challenge causes you gnawing pain, or the thought of making it happen lights you up from within, then that is a sign to focus on that. If, however, other items on your Adversity Inventory score higher on the pain and excitement meter, then that is your indication to focus on those.

No matter which option you select, you want to be obsessed with the question "What can I do to convert this adversity to some advantage that benefits me and others?" You will get the most out of the pages that follow if you have a specific goal or goals in mind. You'll capture your best ideas and then hone them to your first steps, culminating in your Everyday Greatness Game Plan. I encourage you to write down your insights and bright ideas, because you are going to use them in your Game Plan shortly.

Summit One: Take It On!

Begin by choosing either the Singular Challenge or the Multiple Challenge. Decide now and apply all that follows to your choice.

What's the most compelling reason for taking on this adversity (or these adversities)? If you don't have a compelling reason, you probably won't prevail. What's the why beneath the why that drives you to take this on? What is the deeper reason this really matters to you?

On the basis of all that you've learned, jot down your best thoughts about how you could harness the adversity in a way that not only reduces your pain and achieves some goal, but also elevates others in the process. As an Adversity Alchemist, how will you turn that adversity into something good?

As you think about your challenge, consider how you could move up the Adversity Continuum. For example, if you are stuck on the level of Managing Adversity, how could you move up to the top level, Harnessing Adversity? What excuses have you made in the past that prevented you from taking it on? Are any Adversity Assumptions holding you back?

Summit Two: Summon Your Strengths

As you consider your challenge, how can you Summon Your Strengths to deliver greatness? What strengths do you currently possess that will serve you best in relation to that challenge? What strengths do you need to develop?

Beyond your Regular Strengths, what Adversity Strengths do

you possess that you can employ on this challenge in a way that elevates others? If you had to focus on one or two such strengths, which would you select as *most* important?

How strong is your Will? For which challenge(s) do you have the greatest will to Take It On and create some advantage? Remember, if you lack the will, you won't.

Who needs to be "on rope" with you to take on this challenge? Who should *not* be on your team? What strengths do you need from your team members in order to achieve your goal? Who brings the right combination of AWE: A Factor (strength with adversity), W Factor (a compelling why), and the E Factor (a healthy, substantiated ego)?

Summit Three: Engage Your CORE

As you consider this challenge, how can you Engage Your CORE in a way that strengthens and inspires the people around you? Specifically, how will it affect you, and others, when you consciously engage your CORE to respond more effectively?

For any challenge, ask yourself the CORE questions:

- ▸ What facets of this situation can I potentially influence? (C)
- ▸ What can I do to affect this situation immediately and positively? (O)
- ▸ How can I contain this adversity? How can I minimize the downside? What can I do to optimize the potential upside? (R)
- ▸ How can I get through this as quickly as possible? (E)

Imagine what life will look like after you surmount this adversity. Engage in Energy Lending and borrow some positive energy from your vision of the future.

Summit Four: Pioneer Possibilities

What challenge would most people consider impossible, but would change the game if you made it possible? What can't you currently do? And if you could, how would you do it? Are you focusing on the right challenge? What Worthy Goal sparks your *motivation, strength*, and *excitement*?

You will recall that adversity is the perfect force to tap your deeper reserves of innovation and ingenuity. When lacking the tools or means to accomplish what must be done, Possibility Pioneers invent them, often using whatever sparse resources they have available at the time. What Signature Systems can you cobble together to make the unlikely happen? How can you Practice to Perfect?

Summit Five: Pack Light, Pack Right

One of the greatest impediments to giving your challenges the focus, energy, and resources they require is the natural tendency to get distracted and burdened by life. It's easy to slip into the role of obligation martyr and rob yourself of the life force it will take to be an Adversity Alchemist who delivers greatness, every day.

So, how can you Pack Light and Pack Right by better focusing your time, money, and energy on things that generate the greatest Life Worth (the value you and others get from and give to life)? How can you spring-clean your stuff, your calendar, and your relationships so you can redirect your resources toward the things that matter most? What do you need to toss out or reduce? What do you need to reposition to the front of your life, and what needs to be added? If you had three bins labeled "Toss," "Keep," and "Add," what obligations and commitments would go in which bin?

How well do you invest your time in better health and overall well-being? If you had to strengthen one area of your health and capacity—spiritual, mental, emotional, or physical—which one would you choose, and why? What is one simple way you can bring it back to life?

Summit Six: Suffer Well

The path to achieving most elevating goals involves some degree of suffering. And while it is unpleasant, at best, that's a good thing. You can suffer poorly, or you can Suffer Well. Use your pain to fuel your ascent, and as a high-powered opportunity to elevate others.

Being brutally honest with yourself, in what ways are you likely to suffer? In the past, how would those who know you best describe how you tended to suffer? What changes do you need to make to ensure that, as you pursue this challenge, you Suffer Well? Specifically, how can you shoulder the full force of the adversity in a way that elevates and perhaps earns the genuine admiration of the people around you?

Crafting Your Game Plan

The next steps are simple, but important. You will want to copy the following form on a piece of paper. Then you will use all that you have learned and listed to insert your best thoughts and ideas. The most important thing is to give your Game Plan your finest effort. The more thoughtful and specific you are, the greater your likelihood of gaining the fullest possible advantage from your adversities.

ADVERSITY ADVANTAGE:
EVERYDAY GREATNESS GAME PLAN

MY SUMMIT CHALLENGE
The challenge I choose to take on first is:

_____

MY ADVERSITY CHALLENGE
The greatest adversity I will face is:

_____

THE SUMMIT
When I successfully convert this adversity to an advantage, the ways I will benefit include:

_____

The ways others will likely benefit include:

_____

MY STRENGTHS
I have, and will draw upon, the following Adversity Strengths:

_____

I will develop the following Adversity Strengths:

_____

MY ROPE TEAM
I need people on my team who can supply these Adversity Strengths:

_____

The person, or people, I want with me are:

_____

MY STRATEGY
My initial approach will be to:

_____

I commit to get started no later than:

_____

The first step of this plan will be completed by:

_____

Putting Greatness into Action

You now hold your Everyday Greatness Game Plan in your hand. But, to unleash its true force, you must also hold it in your heart. And that may be the remaining challenge. Do you, *can* you, fully comprehend what you are about to unleash? Erik and I believe that, if you did, you would let nothing get in the way of putting your Game Plan into immediate motion.

Most likely you have read books designed to help you strengthen yourself, your team, your relationships, and your organization. This may not be the first time you emerge from a book with some sort of action plan, some of which you may have actually implemented. And that may be just fine. But this Game Plan is entirely different.

We wrote this book to show you the powerful difference between wrestling adversity into submission or conquering it for your own satisfaction, and using adversity to elevate yourself and the lives of those around you. It is about the vital role adversity plays in helping you become the kind of leader you aspire to be, and that means growing your organization, driving your team forward, or helping your family thrive, all in the harshest weather.

Your relationship with adversity drives everything in your life. It is utterly foundational to all you aspire to be and do. As Stephen Covey points out in his eloquent foreword, these teachings can fuel a noble, principle-centered life. So, done right, your Game Plan can infuse greatness into every facet of your world. In fact, our positive warning is this: *Greatness is potently contagious*. Once unleashed, it can readily take root and flourish in what would be otherwise lifeless soil. What if the people around you were also striving to employ the *Adversity Advantage* principles to deliver greatness every day? Can you imagine the impact that could have on your family or your team or your business?

While each person's journey through this book is highly personal, I hope you have already strengthened your relationship with adversity so that you can begin to use it as a true advantage in your life. This book is intended to help you use life's hardest moments for the most uplifting pursuits. It is about your new role as an Adversity Alchemist, converting life's tough stuff into the rich ore of everyday greatness.

To help elevate your thinking regarding what's possible once you unleash your Everyday Greatness Game Plan, we leave you with this final story, in Erik's words, of how a humble life from anywhere in the world and all the lives within its current and future reach can be forever transformed when *The Adversity Advantage* principles and tools are put to good use.

Erik

Blindsight

It wasn't until I met Sabriye Tenberken that I learned her amazing story. She is from Bonn, Germany. Similar to me, she had been blinded at age twelve by a degenerative retinal disease. But she didn't let that tragedy kill her vision. She saw herself making a positive difference in the world. So, instead of merely coping with her adversity, she stepped out to make her mark. Sabriye first applied to a government-funded program to help underprivileged people in other parts of the world. But the German government flatly denied her application, making it clear that her disability would preclude her from doing such work.

Sabriye remained undaunted. She simply rerouted by taking a keen interest in a neglected spot in the world: Tibet. She earned a master's degree in Tibetology so she'd have some knowledge and skill to support her mission. When she discovered that there was no Braille alphabet for Tibetan—a complex language based on forty-two syllables—she developed one in just two weeks. As she explains, "It was a matter of necessity. I had picked Tibet as the country where I wanted to do development work. Because a Braille system didn't exist, I needed to create one."

Creating the Braille alphabet was just the beginning. Sabriye's biggest challenges were yet to come. Although Tibet is widely regarded as a mountain paradise, its people suffer twice the rate of blindness per capita as the global average, largely due to high altitude and sun exposure, coupled with the constant soot from yak dung used as fuel for their fires. (The proportion of blind Tibetans is one in seventy.) Blind Tibetan children are considered cursed with demons, and their blindness is regarded as a punishment to the family for misdeeds by someone in their lineage in a previous life.

In 1997, after scraping together her meager resources, Sabriye entered Tibet with just herself and her cane. Then she did a most courageous thing. Accompanied by a Tibetan health counselor, she traveled the rigorous mountain countryside on horseback to check on the plight of the blind. Despite her warm heart and good intentions, she received a cold reception.

"It was depressing," she explained. "We met kids who had been tied to beds for years so they didn't hurt themselves. Some couldn't walk because their parents hadn't given them the space to develop." When she told me that, it felt like a knife in my heart. Like Sabriye, I couldn't help but hurt for every disabled kid in Tibet who'd been marginalized by ignorance and myth.

While in Lhasa, Sabriye met her future partner, Paul Kronenberg, a development aid worker and a brilliant engineer. Together they took on the tangle of red tape they knew had to be unraveled in order to make progress. In Paul, Sabriye found a teammate who supplemented her strengths. Together they could achieve what she could not do alone.

Sabriye faced countless setbacks and refusals, using each to fuel her perseverance and vision. Finally, in May 1998, she opened Braille Without Borders, the first training center for blind and visually impaired children in Lhasa. She started with only three students, facing enormous prejudice and superstition, as well as bureaucratic resistance. Over the following years, however, Sabriye laid the foundation for the now-respected school.

She taught her students to independently navigate the chaotic city of Lhasa with their canes. When they faced ridicule in the streets, she taught them to fight back with their words. She taught them to use special computers with voice synthesizers, and most important, she taught them to never be ashamed of their blindness. Ten years later, enrollment was up to 135 students.

It was a year after my Mount Everest climb that I received a life-changing letter from Sabriye.

> Dear Erik,
>
> After you have reached the top of the world our Tibetan neighbour rushed into our center and told the kids about your success. Some of them first didn't believe it, but then there was a mutual understanding: if you could climb to the top of the world, we also can overcome our barriers and show to the world that the blind can equally participate in society and are able to accomplish great things. . . . The children realized that it does not matter much if you are a blind child in Germany, USA or Tibet, the experience one has who becomes blind, the embarrassment at first, the confidence which builds up slowly but steadily, the reaction of the sighted surrounding is probably for every blind person the same . . .

Sabriye wrote to invite me to visit her school. But I thought I could do more. Why not take the students on an Everest-sized adventure—something that no one in their families, no one in their villages, had ever done? The Everest region has such deep spiritual, symbolic, mythical importance in their culture, I thought it would be immeasurably powerful to bring them there. I wanted these children to know they were special, to feel a part of something big. I hoped that the "bigness" of such an expedition would ingrain itself inside them and affect the rest of their lives.

PHOTOGRAPH BY DIDRIK JOHNCK

On my first trip to Tibet to train the six blind Tibetan teenagers for our Climbing Blind expedition, I wondered if the kids were tough enough to succeed. My question was answered when they playfully wrestled me to the ground and nearly succeeded in hog-tying me with our spare climbing rope.

So, I asked Sabriye to pick the six students she thought would be best suited to our challenge and, along with some friends from my Mount Everest climb, headed on a plane to Lhasa, Tibet. On our first visit, we took the kids on a training trek, with lots of coaching. It ended up being an arduous ascent up and over a 17,500-foot pass. The students struggled, and some got sick, but we made it. Their will was steadfast, and their skills evolved quickly as the challenge intensified.

We came back several months later with the goal of guiding these six blind kids to a peak on the East Rongbuk Glacier, a huge glacial formation on the north side of Everest, just above the 21,000-foot camp. Along the way, we confronted difficult trails and brutally cold temperatures. Some moments were pretty scary, such as when one child fell into a crevasse. But we were roped together, so he was immediately hauled out. We even had to traverse a mini-icefall—riddled with serpentine columns of ice, jutting pinnacles, and shifting shards—by following a zigzagging pathway through the labyrinth. The kids had never experienced anything like this before. The experience was incredibly tactile, filling them with wonder as they played in that magical palace of ice.

Our expedition took almost a month. Many of the kids got sick from the altitude. All of them struggled. But ultimately, these blind Tibetan teens, who had been hit with rocks, sold into slavery, and tied to beds in dark rooms, all stood at 21,500 feet, higher than any team of blind people in history.

At our high point, there wasn't much of a dramatic celebration. The kids were pretty tired and seemed kind of ambivalent about our achievement—even stunned. So on the way down, I was privately wondering if I had done the right thing. Had I just put them through unnecessary suffering?

It was on my last day in Tibet that the six Tibetan kids all gathered around me at the training center. Kyila, who had the best English of the group, spoke on behalf of the others: "We all want to know if you will come back to take us to the top of Mount Everest?"

"I thought you didn't like climbing?" I asked playfully.

"We love climbing!" they all yelled incredulously.

"You can't climb mountains," I teased. "You're blind."

"We can do anything," our tiniest team member, Sonom Bonsu, shot back, and she proceeded to haul off and punch me in the arm.

"We want to climb higher," Kyila said.

Since then, their aspirations have grown. Kyila, after studying in the United Kingdom for a year, took over running the day-to-day management of the Braille Without Borders school. Gyenshen started the first Braille printing business in Tibet. Sonom Bonsu graduated first in her class at her sighted school. Two more from the group now run the biggest massage therapy clinic in Lhasa.

Once some of Sabriye's students were approached by nomads who had never seen a cane before. The nomads began to laugh and ridicule the teens, calling them blind fools. One blind boy turned to face them and said, "You cannot talk to me like that. I am blind, but I am not a fool! Did you ever go to school? Do you know how to read and write? Can you find the toilet in the middle of the night without a flashlight?"

Recently, another group of her students were confronted by a pack of sighted boys. Gearing up for a fight, the blind students faced off, but to their surprise, one of the sighted boys said, "You seem so happy. You go to such a good school. You must be lucky. I wish I were blind."

Sabriye Tenberken and her young blind students have turned blindness on its head. Just a short time ago these young people were the outcasts of society. Now their blindness gives them strength, and propels them forward with determination and joy.

The spirit of these young blind Tibetans was so infectious that when I got home, I wanted to do more. Why weren't blind kids from America being exposed to these big adventures? The answer is Leading the Way, a program founded in partnership with an outstanding nonprofit organization, Global Explorers. Each summer, we take integrated teams of blind and sighted teenagers on educational experiences around the world. So far, we've trekked the Inca Trail in Peru, explored the Amazon rain forest, and rafted the Grand Canyon.

One of our American blind team members had a story that reminded

Despite cold, wind, rocky trails, crevasses, and altitude sickness, our young Tibetan team members reached 21,500 feet on the north face of Mount Everest. Young people who were told they had evil spirits inside them, were tied to beds in dark rooms, and were sold into slavery ultimately stood higher than any team of blind people in history.

me of the Tibetan students. While his parents were at work, he was restricted to the house and his room, forbidden even from walking to the end of his driveway to get the mail. His school counselor made a hard sell to his parents for him to join us. At the end of a rugged, seven-day hike across the Andes, he turned to me, sweaty and exhausted, and said, "Erik, I wouldn't exactly say that was fun, but it's changed my life."

So one blind German girl decides she wants to grow up and make a difference. Like anyone trying to do something worthwhile, she faces immense adversity along the way. But, being an alchemist, she converts that adversity into the rich ore of everyday greatness, equipping young children with the same principles you've learned in this book, so they can create their own brand of greatness for generations to come. That is Sabriye's legacy.

You'll recall that sixteen years ago, while climbing in Arizona, my buddy turned to me and, out of the blue, said, "What do you say we try something a little bigger?" which began a quest that carried me around the world, confronting some of life's greatest challenges. And along the way, I learned that a spark of greatness exists in all people, but only by touching that spark to adversity's flame does it blaze into the force that fuels our lives and the world.

That's my story of *The Adversity Advantage.*

What's yours?

Acknowledgments

First and foremost, we would like to express our deepest gratitude to our editorial team: Ed Weihenmayer, Tina Shultz, Jeff Thompson, Mike Savicki, and especially Nellie Sabin, who is chiefly responsible for this new edition. Special thanks to our amazing wives, Ellie and Ronda, who signed up for this lifelong "climb" and sacrificed their rest and sanity on many endless late-night read-throughs. We thank our valued clients and teams, without whom many of these principles would remain untested; our gifted publishers, Nancy Hancock and Trish Grader, and their team at Fireside; as well as our expert agent, Denise Marcil, at the Denise Marcil Agency. We also wish to express particular gratitude to one of the great men of our time, Dr. Stephen Covey, through whose principles and generosity this book and its authors are immeasurably improved. Without the extended faith, dedication, and sacrifice of all these exceptional people, along with their proven ability to put these practices into action, *The Adversity Advantage* might never have reached the printed page.

Index

About the Authors

ERIK WEIHENMAYER is a celebrated athlete and the only blind person in history to climb the Seven Summits. His memoir, *Touch the Top of the World*, is printed in eight languages and was made into a feature film. Erik is the subject of the award-winning documentaries *Farther than the Eye Can See* and *Blindsight*. He has been featured on the cover of *Time*, *Outside*, and *Climbing* magazines. Erik speaks to audiences on harnessing life's challenges to find the greatness within us. Through his mountaineering adventures, speaking engagements, and outreach programs, Erik has traveled to more than fifty countries around the globe, not only from the top of Mount Everest to the jungles of New Guinea, but also from the 2005 APEC Summit in Chile to the 2009 Presidential Inaugural Celebration in Washington, D.C. He lives with his family in the Rocky Mountains.

For more information on Erik, go to touchthetop.com. To see a video clip of Erik speaking about harnessing adversity, go to adversityadvantage.com.

- ▶ To learn more about No Barriers, a nonprofit organization that teaches people with challenges the innovative ideas, techniques, and technologies that can help them live more adventurous lives, go to nobarriersusa.org.
- ▶ To learn more about Leading the Way, Erik's project that takes integrated teams of blind and sighted teenagers on leadership and team-building adventures around the world, go to globalexplorers.org.
- ▶ To learn more about the Kilimanjaro Blind Trust, which promotes Braille literacy for blind children throughout East Africa, go to kilimanjaro-blindtrust.org.
- ▶ To learn more about Braille Without Borders, the Lhasa-based training center for blind Tibetans founded by Sabriye Tenberken, go to braillewithoutborders.org.

PAUL G. STOLTZ, PH.D., is the CEO of PEAK Learning, a global research and consulting firm; and the director of the Global Resilience Project. The originator of the globally acclaimed Adversity Quotient (AQ) method and author of the international bestseller *Adversity Quotient* and *Adversity Quotient at Work*, he lives in San Luis Obispo, California. For more information regarding Dr. Paul Stoltz, Adversity Quotient (AQ), or the PEAK Learning suite of assessments, products, keynotes, programs, coaching, and consulting solutions, go to peaklearning.com, or contact PEAK directly at info@peaklearning.com or (805) 595-7775.